Eggplant Rufus

Tiger Taylor

*Amused Indifference
on a Stupid Planet*

*visit www.eggplantrufus.com
...it's important that you do so.*

ISBN – 978-0-9777996-0-2

Acknowledgments

Eggplant Rufus and all that surrounds it is dedicated to two groovey chicks:

(1) My mother – a great mom who has shown you are never too old or too young to enjoy your life – I'm proud of you lady!

(2) My Mellie - who honored me by taking my name, and was then cool enough to give me another.

COVER CREDITS:

And lest I forget, many thanks to the hugely talented Matt Reed for his brilliant efforts in designing the cover for this book and his continued magnificent work on www.eggplantrufus.com. Get your ass over to that website and check out what this man can do.
No excuses!

About the Author

Tiger Taylor was born in 1963.

Tiger is a nickname awarded to the author a few moments after birth – the nurse on duty, after dealing with kicking and random peeing – noted, "You have a real tiger here." Later, when the author attended college, he was introduced to the poetry of William Blake and his figurehead work "The Tyger." This particular poem features some awful rhymes, but remains overall a funky piece and in the end, that's good enough. It's a great poem because on the surface, you might think it is just about a tiger. But when you analyze it over and over again, you come up with dozens of additional meanings that provide insights into emotions, mortality and man's sense of self. These additional meanings when placed end-to-end are ultimately less interesting than just a poem about a tiger.

Taylor was the name of the hapless astronaut in Pierre Boulle's novel "Planet of the Apes." Here's the deal with Taylor – he puts himself to sleep in a space capsule hurtling through the universe one day and wakes up to find himself crash landing on an alien planet. It turns out that the group in power on that planet consists of a collection of gorillas - and damned unpleasant ones at that. He finds a couple of apes who help him out along the way, and a mute, barely-dressed chick to tag along and make out with when he is bored. Ultimately, he sees a wrecked Statue of Liberty on the beach and comes to the unhappy realization that he is on Earth a few years later than when he left it in his rocket ship.

If that's confusing, just ask yourself how many times you have wondered whether or not you are on some kind of "planet of the apes?" If you don't ask yourself this question on almost a daily basis, then perhaps you are, in fact, one of the apes.

Table of Contents

A Brief Introduction to Eggplant Rufus...

Conversation with a Stranger 1

Sack on a Nail 3

Ed's Kid Blows Up the World 5

Urinal Pucks..7

Girly Fights 9

Alpha Cilantro.. 11

Struck By Lightning 13

Big American Weiners 15

Kitten Heads... 17

Neptune the Ape Woman... 19

Strip Mall Still Life 21

Handful of Wishes 23

Life Ain't Metaphorical.. 25

My Cubicle, My Castle 27

Goat Knowledge.. 29

Vietnam... 30

Underpants Wisdom... 32

Mrs. Peters' Peanut Butter.. 33

Puzzle for Penance 35

Green Curry Epiphany 37

Tubbie in a Tavern 39

Heaven 41

Boogers 43

Frank's New Attitude 45

Yard Balls 47

Brains on Tiananmen Square 48

Most Beautiful Woman 50

Drink Restoration 52

Spider on a White Wall 53

Cold Meat Loaf Sandwiches 55

Tight Game 57

One Hundred Years Hence 58

Funeral Pies 60

In Debt 62

Esther's Hooters 64

Yohnee Bopping 66

Condoms 68

Twenty Thousand Dead Chicks 70

Amanda Behind Glass 72

Four Dimes in Your Pocket.. 74

Infected Butt.. 76

Witness Protection Program.. 78

Think Tank 80

Mansions of Rhode Island... 82

By the Side of the Road 84

Autumn in New York 86

Chickens on the Beach 88

Tight Blue Dresses.. 90

Yard Sale Saturday.. 92

Kamikaze Argument 94

Hairbrush Microphone 96

Deja Moo.. 98

Friend in Space 100

Bowling Night 102

Broccoli Feedback 104

Hateful Chapin 106

Mildred's Magic Carpet 108

Macaroni Snow 110

Sweet Perspective 112

Clouds 114

Hair Salon Soliloquy 116

Old Man at McDonald's...118

Buffet Virtuosos 120

Hammertoe 122

Happier Days 124

Mouse Suicide Note 126

Pepperoni Optimism 127

Midnight in La Jolla 129

Potato Salad..131

Dead Crap Trilogy 133

Sea Monkeys and Corned Beef Hash 135

Throw a Bone...137

Cicada Vacation 139

Manhattan Krishna...141

Lucy's Lucky Lighter 143

Buy More Eggplant 146

A Brief Introduction to Eggplant Rufus

You are about to read seventy-five little stories that may or may not hold your interest – they were mildly interesting to me when I wrote them, but I certainly have no idea if you will have the same opinion. You are likely to read some of these and wonder, "Why would anyone write that?" Another potential question might be, "What the hell was that all about?"

I think these are very natural and healthy responses. Don't be alarmed. I can't help what I write – very much like some people cannot control an urge, or others might fart out loud in the middle of a serious conversation. And just like that individual who interrupts his discourse with unexpected flatulence, I don't apologize for any of this – I am just going to keep going, one after the other.

One piece of business I can clear up is the significance of the title – "Eggplant Rufus." I have been asked on several occasions, "What does it mean?" Here is your answer: Nothing. I was sitting in my living room listening to a Lou Reed album sometime in the late 1980's and in a song entitled "The Beginning of a Great Adventure," he randomly listed perhaps one hundred names for his soon-to-be-born son. "Eggplant" and "Rufus" were two of those names and he recited them consecutively in the song.

At that moment in my life, I happened to be staring at a stack of poetry that I wanted to turn into a little book. The collection was so devoid of a common theme that I had no idea what to call it. Then Lou Reed sang those names.

Thus "Eggplant Rufus" was born. It was a moment in which my timing and location collided to put me in the right situation to hear the perfect title for my book. And when it was all said and done, it was and remains almost meaningless. Maybe there in itself could be a theme for the book you are about to read – and perhaps a description that is suitable enough for all of the little stories that follow.

So begin your journey through the twisted landscape of "Eggplant Rufus" and my seventy-five "farts during conversation." I hope occasionally the timing and location in your life might coincide so that one or two of them make you smile and say, "What the hell was that all about?"

Wherever possible, Enjoy.

Conversation with a Stranger

I had a conversation with a fellow today,

One of those brief exchanges with someone

That you really don't like

Where they take that single opportunity

To wrap up all of their feelings on issues

You never asked them about.

It was women today,

The topic of discussion in our private three-minute session

And he rambled on about how you can't trust them

Further than you can throw a Cadillac –

They're all the same and only rise above one another by comparison

Of their flaws.

He talked about his laundry list of failures

And how every one had been because of some lying

Untrustable bitch

Who had been pole-vaulted from the depths of Hell

For a slightly longer period of time than is necessary

To make his life miserable.

It was God's earthly payback for repeatedly using the Creator's

Name in vain and for shoplifting a pack of chewing gum

From a drug store in 1971.

There were, according to him, only two decent women on Earth –

One was already married to his father and the other,

Realizing her status as the other remaining decent female on the planet,

Eggplant Rufus

Had a sex change to become what she should have been
All along.
I looked in his eyes as he continued and I knew he didn't believe
A word he was saying.
That somewhere along the way this whining character
Had probably run into a satanic hell-beast or two,
But more than likely he had done most of the damage himself.
Blame is therapeutic,
A cheap tonic that allows the user to proceed
Without the rigors of self-analysis and all you need to feel better
Is to have one helpless, unsuspecting bastard
Listen to you while you dribble out your list of excuses.
Today that helpless bastard was me and,
After a moment of silence when I just looked into his eyes,
I knew this experience was finally over
And the meager therapy I could provide for this appointment
Was complete.
I wiped the shaving cream off my face with an old towel,
Looked in the mirror one more time
And thought about what I was going to wear to work.

Sack on a Nail

The camp counselor came into our cabin just before lights out

And gave us a quick but educational lecture about

Horseplay

In our bunks.

There were a dozen or so ten year-olds in every cabin,

And that meant at least six young boys perched in the upper bunk

Each night during our two weeks at summer camp.

There was the inevitable temptation for any adolescent male

In such a precarious position

To commit acts of senseless, boyish fun.

Thus the counselor was forewarning each of us of the potential

Consequences,

By reciting the tale of a young boy who committed just such

Wild indiscretions only a year before at that very camp.

He had apparently proclaimed that he could jump from his top bunk

To the floor,

And upon doing so was completely successful.

However, during his flight to the ground,

His testicles became tangled on a two-penny nail

Pounded into the side of the top bunk,

And just as surely as that counselor stood before us,

So did that young camper's balls hang dangling from that nail

Like fuzzy dice from a rear view mirror.

So let his misfortune be a lesson learned for all of us,

Eggplant Rufus

And each bunk in the cabin had its own jutting nail

Waiting to ensnare our own ballsacks should we attempt

Any tomfoolery.

The counselor shut off the light,

And left us sitting silently in our bunks

Waiting for sleep.

I, being one of the unfortunate top bunk residents,

Now held tightly to both sides of the bed and tried desperately

To position my genitals between my thighs in case I should roll accidentally

During a dream later in the evening.

It was a long and fitful night's sleep,

And almost a full three nights more before I and every other boy in the cabin

Began jumping

From those top bunks.

Ed's Kid Blows Up the World

Ed bought his kid an Erector set

For his birthday.

It was the biggest, fanciest model

With every conceivable shape and angle

And battery-powered motors

To make any completed project move.

It was a nifty set,

But Ed's kid was a mean little son-of-a-bitch,

And spent four consecutive days in his room

Constructing a doomsday device which could

Eradicate the western hemisphere

And begin a chain reaction that would send the Earth

Hurtling out of orbit

Until it exploded in a fiery ball

In the atmosphere of the Sun.

It would have worked too,

Except for the moment that Ed's kid decided to set off the contraption

And thus eliminate life on Earth as we know it,

His sister called him into the living room

To tell him

That the Teenage Mutant Ninja Turtles

Were on the television.

Then,

While both kids sat silently glued to the cartoon,

Eggplant Rufus

Ed's wife took the batteries from the Erector set

To place in the vibrator which she used as a surrogate Ed

While the real Ed was on the road for days at a time

To make the money to buy the biggest, fanciest Erector sets

For a son who – unknown to Ed – was the most dangerous

Human being on the face of the planet.

When the episode of the Ninja Turtles was over,

Ed's kid calmly walked into his room

And pressed the little red button

In the middle of the device.

There was no blinking, no ticking, no movement

Of tiny Erector gears

That would set in motion the child-made apocalypse.

The boy scratched his head,

And like any adolescent dealing with a malfunctioning creation,

Smashed the doomsday device to bits with a baseball bat.

Thus,

Ed's kid really hasn't blown up the world,

Yet.

Urinal Pucks

I pay homage to you

Oh pink and white discs of delight!

All freshness and calm

With you on the job,

Perched sentry-like

In the depths of a urinal.

We exchange glances

Then mutely go about our business.

I am here for a reason

And so most assuredly are you.

My purpose as I stand is to create the odors

You so laboriously obscure.

Oh urinal pucks,

You serve us well

And give every last fiber of your being

Until the inevitable dissolution

Of the last tiny

Speck

Of your soul.

Like snowflakes,

No two urinal pucks are alike,

But your replacement will most certainly share

Your stoic dedication to duty

And your eternal kinship

Eggplant Rufus

With mankind:

You and I, urinal puck,

Both of us

Pissed on every day

Until we finally

Disappear.

Girly Fights

Walking home from school as a boy,

I remember that hair-standing-on-the-back-of-your-neck

Excitement

That would follow the high-pitched wailing and passionate shrieking

Announcing the commencement of a first-rate girly fight.

Who knows how it all got started,

Surely someone infringed on someone's territory or

Perhaps the disagreement born at least weekend's

Slumber party

Had festered through the school days and matured

Into fisticuffs.

Who knows what causes a subtle disagreement to escalate

Into a full-throttle girly fight,

But it's a beautiful thing to watch.

In reality, the underlying reason for the flare up is inconsequential

Once hair starts being pulled.

Today there are flailing arms, wrists slapping necks and foreheads and ribs

And both combatants have been crying since the opening bell.

Finally, a technical knockout is achieved

When a hair pull yields a clump of brunette threads and a slab

Of freshly torn scalp.

The loser runs home with her hands over her head

Screaming incomprehensibly,

While the winner seems awed and visibly shaken by the grisly Consequences

Of her triumph.

Those of us gathered around are moved by the gruesome scene to shout

"Best girly fight ever!"

Later, parents will be called,

Apologies will be offered,

Perhaps even gifts exchanged.

But the memory of this auspicious girly fight will linger

And the next day everyone will walk behind the loser at one point or another

To see if the hole in her scalp is visible to the naked eye.

They were both brave warriors that day,

Now faded away through the decades like photographs in an album

Best left tucked away in a closet.

But for those of us who observed,

Those of we fortunate few who had the great convergence of

Timing and proximity to see this timeless event,

We'll always recall that rush of adrenaline when you first hear the cries,

The mass mentality of the cheering crowd overwhelmed by the

That wonderful surprise that results

When a normally routine walk home from school

Includes as a bonus a front row ticket

To a full-blown

Girly fight.

Alpha Cilantro

It is December of 1986 and I am sitting on a second story rooftop bar

In Tijuana, Mexico.

On the street below there are children chasing pennies,

And donkeys just days from being dead dragged from block to block.

To my left I can see an old bullfighting ring,

And a small shop that advertises divorces for ten dollars.

This is an interesting place to be sure.

I am drinking a semi-warm Mexican beer

When the waiter brings a small basket of nacho chips and a bowl of salsa.

It is an enormous bowl of salsa, actually, and I am at first struck by the fact

That he must believe I will drink it like gazpacho.

I lower a chip into the tomato-strewn liquid and take a bite.

Suddenly, a new taste overwhelms me.

At first, I am certain that something is wrong,

Maybe the salsa has been sitting out too long in the hot Mexican sun.

But ultimately, I trace the source of this new sensation

To tiny flecks of chopped green leaves that are floating in the bowl.

I ask the waiter what on earth these could be,

And he informs that they are pieces of cilantro.

Mexican parsley.

Holy shit, I am thinking to myself,

I am sitting across from a place where you can divorce your spouse

For a ten spot,

And I am now being exposed to cilantro for the first time.

Eggplant Rufus

I am twenty-three years old in Tijuana, Mexico,

The air is hot, and I am now glad that I have this gigantic bowl of salsa

Overloaded with this new incredible weed to delight my senses.

A year later, on the outskirts of London, Ontario,

I would have a similar episode experiencing capers for the first time.

No one can describe the taste of a caper to you,

It tastes like no other food on Earth.

A friend I was with on this journey indicated that it was his belief that

Capers tasted like ass.

It's apparent now that if this gentleman is even near being accurate

In his description,

Then I most certainly like the taste of ass,

Because I became quite addicted to capers that cold night in Canada.

Today, now many years later,

I am eating a sea bass lightly grilled sitting outside on the deck of a Restaurant

Overlooking the Pacific Ocean in Del Mar, California.

The fish is cooked perfectly with a delicate sauce that features

Cilantro and capers.

With a southern California sunset dancing over the waves,

I am experiencing in my mouth memories from two decades before

And thinking fondly

Of ten-dollar divorces, dilapidated donkeys

And the magnificent taste of ass.

Struck By Lightning

Ricardo had a good life, he thought, and didn't know why he ever

Communicated with an internet psychic, but the day that he did she told Him

That he would soon meet a beautiful woman and she would say "yes"

If he asked her out on a date.

And it happened, just as the psychic had said.

The following day the same psychic informed him that he would get a job

Promotion and sure enough, this also occurred completely out of the blue.

So imagine his horror when on the third day,

His newfound advisor was hesitant in her words to him:

"I don't want to tell you what I see."

He needed to know, she had been accurate so consistently, he must know.

"I see you being struck by lightning," she said.

So he stayed at home, now fearful of stepping outside.

He would email her every day, and she would say again,

"I see you being struck by lightning."

He was fired from his job because he did not show up for work,

He began ordering all of his food through the internet and

Communicated only through email and his computer -

He could not use the telephone because he had heard lightning bolts

Can travel through phone lines.

Finally his savings were gone and he had no money for internet groceries.

He tried everything he could do on the web to try and earn some extra cash,

Even registering for every internet sweepstakes in existence.

It was to no avail, and soon he was a frail and scraggly version of what he

Eggplant Rufus

Once was and now crawling from room to room in his home.
His internet and electricity were shut off and the home was freezing cold
That day he finally died of exposure and starvation.
His mother flew in from across the country because her son had stopped
Emailing her and his last communications seemed desperate.
The house was filthy when she used a key under the mat to gain entrance,
And found her son lying dead on the kitchen floor.
He was emaciated and his hair had not been clipped in a year,
What had gone wrong?
She broke down and cried as someone knocked on the door -
There were seven men with balloons and a large check standing outside
And they were alarmed when the woman did not shriek with delight
At the news they had to tell her.
When she told them her son had recently died,
And would not be able to enjoy the sixty million dollars he had won
In the world's largest internet sweepstakes,
They wrapped their arms around her to comfort her,
To provide any consolation they could.
"I know this does not help at all, but your son would have been a very
Happy man if he were alive today," they said.
"He has won the largest internet sweepstakes every conducted,
The odds of winning are the same as the chances of being
Struck by lightning."

Big American Weiners

Again, as I open my emails on a rainy Tuesday morning,

I am confronted with the notion that

My weiner is not big enough.

From the subject lines of countless spam communications

I am told my wife doesn't really love me and hides her disappointment

Because my weiner isn't the size of a baseball bat.

For thirty dollars a month I can purchase pills

That can increase the size of my weiner by five inches

In only three months.

I am thinking by extrapolation, then, if I took these pills for a year

Would my weiner be twenty inches longer?

If I was on the program for five years

Would the result be that my weiner measured an additional

One hundred inches?

At this point, we are talking about an eight-foot weiner,

Enough to make my penis on its own a highly paid center

In the National Basketball Association.

I look down the road twenty years

To a nation of gigantic and problematic wieners –

How could you get on a plane

Or buy a pair of jeans?

Would Levis and Wrangler have to concoct a third extension sleeve

In the crotch of their denim garments to accommodate

These new enormous wieners?

And those wives that were the original motivation

For this genital augmentation

Would have to accept that their partners

Have to stand in another room

During their intimate moments.

There would certainly be money to be made in such a world:

Surely some capitalist opportunists would sell advertising

On their elongated genitalia,

And undoubtedly the latex industry would boom

As a result of the gargantuan sleeves necessary

To provide prophylactic protection

To these lengthy trouser pipes.

Only in the United States, I am thinking on this stormy Tuesday,

The home of the free

And the land of the big American weiner.

Kitten Heads

Holy smokes – it's a new day in America.

Hardly had enough time to catch my breath from yesterday

And it's a new one already.

Go figure.

Even the most sour pessimist can't help but grin at the breaking dawn.

Jeepers, what a sight!

Somewhere across the world it is probably dark and cold as hell.

Never understood that... "cold as hell."

But here it is all fuzzy and warm like a little kitten.

You want to pick that kitten up in your arms

And squeeze it with all your strength.

Embrace the dawn...

Squeeze its guts out like seeds from a cherry tomato.

My friend had a cousin who would bury kittens

Up to their necks in the back yard.

That's not even the worst part.

After burying them, he would run his dad's riding mower over top of them.

Clip them like dandelions and laugh.

This kid was demented.

This kid grew up and became the head of a major American corporation –

A chairman I think.

He is fiercely competitive,

And I always assume he imagines his business competitors are simply

Kittens with their heads ready for mowing.

Eggplant Rufus

America is full of psychotic fucks like this.

In every pursuit – business, education, politics, sports –

And thousands of other

Professions and occupations.

Just look hard enough and you'll find someone who once

Somehow tormented cats when they were kids

And secretly still yearns to do it again.

Go figure.

So some things suck about living in America,

Especially if you are a cat,

But you cannot complain one single bit about the beautiful orange sky

As the dawn turns into morning.

It's a new day in America...hooray!

Take the time to enjoy those moments

When the gentle sky is just opening its eyes,

Think a little about the day to come, and

If you have a cat,

For God's sake

Keep it inside.

There are indeed some crazy bastards out there.

Neptune the Ape Woman

In 1970, I went to a fairground with my mother and sister to see

Sonny and Cher perform live in an evening concert and serenade us

With "I Got You Babe" and tell some jokes to make us laugh.

I was in love with Cher at the time, and although the odds were slim that a

Successful and married twenty-something musical icon would fall

Head over heels for a tow-headed seven-year old,

I was certain that by being in the audience she would at least notice me.

We arrived about two hours early and walked around the fairground

With all of its carnival rides and booths selling cotton candy and popcorn.

A man stood outside of a tent yelling at us as we passed by,

"Step inside and see the amazing Neptune,

The beauty that turns into an ape before your very eyes."

I asked my mother if we could have a look at what this was all about,

And after paying a small fee, we shuffled inside of the tent where perhaps

Fifty other fair-goers were gathered around a large cage on a stage.

Because I was small, we forced our way to the front so that I could see,

And there I was, a mere six feet away from the steel bars that would

Restrain Neptune when and if she would complete her metamorphosis.

After a few more minutes, the lights dimmed to almost darkness

Except a single spotlight on the cage into which entered a woman

More beautiful than Cher and dressed in a tiny blue bikini.

She seemed angry to be in the cage and I couldn't blame her –

Why did such a pretty girl need to be behind bars?

A strobe light twinkled as I watched a forest of hair grow over her body.

Eggplant Rufus

The lights became more intense and members of the audience
Laughed and hooted, but my seven-year old eyes were fixated on the
Unbelievable scene within arm's length of where I stood.
The strobe light switched off leaving only the single spotlight,
And there standing before me was no longer Neptune,
The beauty in a blue bikini, but a full-sized angry Gorilla.
It began tearing at the bars and I clutched my mothers' legs.
I wanted to close my eyes but couldn't, so I was very aware of that moment
When the gorilla bent the bars and leapt out of the cage into the audience.
My eyes widened to saucers and I dashed out of the tent
To the relative safety of a hot dog vendor about one hundred yards away.
When my mother finally caught up to me, she explained it was all a trick,
That people couldn't really turn into apes.
I tried to play it cool and said, "I knew that, I was just hot in that tent."
It was a lie of course, and for whatever reason, that night at the concert
Cher was not quite so beautiful and several times during the show I swear
I saw fur emerging in the fleshy gaps of her sequined dress.
That was long ago, and you might think this chance encounter
With a summertime carnival sideshow might fade to a childhood memory,
But I confess that from that day on I have lived with a nagging paranoia
That every woman I knew would sooner or later turn into a gorilla.
And do you want to know a secret?
Many times they have.

Strip Mall Still Life

My car is parked

Between the entrances to a

K-Mart, a health club and a liquor store.

I watch as a healthy couple exits the fitness club

Aglow with the results of their activities –

He with his racquetball glasses still perched on his nose

And she clinging to her man as tightly

As her form-fitting Adidas workout gear is wrapped

On her torso.

They are beautiful specimens,

And I imagine that although one would expect much of them,

Their plans for the evening might just as easily include

Eating potato chips in bed and falling asleep

While watching network television.

At the same time as they exit the gym,

I look to my right to see a much less attractive couple

Leaving the liquor store with armloads

Of wine, tequila and rum.

They will drink this night until they find each other attractive,

I speculate,

And wrestle though the night in furious coitus.

Simultaneously,

A much older couple

Walks out of the K-mart.

Eggplant Rufus

They are easily in their early eighties

And leave the store with a small bag

Containing the paper towels he will use to clean

The urine his wife will inevitably leave on the sofa

Because he could never imagine

His beautiful best friend

Wearing diapers.

Three couples and three stores

In a strip mall in suburban America.

The song I am listening to on the radio ends and I watch

Them all drive away.

I'll never see them again for the rest of my life,

Or maybe,

I'll see them endlessly and every day,

Everywhere I go.

Handful of Wishes

My old friend Bob was a lobbyist

And a great golfer –

He taught me what suits to wear

And which ties were the classiest

And to always listen to Frank Sinatra.

And one day while we sat eating clams at a local restaurant,

He told me the story of his life and how every time

That he thought he had been completely knocked down and out,

Something good would happen to him

Right out of the blue.

It was just the way things happened.

I asked what his secret was,

Did he have a genie in a lamp to make his wishes come true?

No, he said, he never wished for anything -

He just let it happen.

Wishes are for suckers and he would summarize it thusly:

If you had a handful of wishes in one hand

And a handful of dog feces in the other,

The only thing you could really count on

Was that you would be standing with one hand full of nothing,

And the other hand full of shit.

So, I would think to myself,

It's always better to have clean hands.

A few years later,

Eggplant Rufus

I bought a Dalmatian puppy that could not be trained,

And on one occasion I had just picked up a small pile of poop

She had left behind in the dining room of my house.

It was the same spot where the dog had left similar gifts

Every single day since I brought it home from the kennel.

However, on this day, something stuck me out of the past and

I was jolted into paralysis –

I was transported back in time to that day eating clams with Bob

And talking about wishes.

Now here I was years later,

Standing with an actual pile of dog shit in my right hand –

It seemed the appropriate time to test his theory.

I closed my eyes, made my little wish,

And envisioned it flying like a butterfly from my heart to my

Outstretched left hand.

Thus, both hands were now occupied.

And so it came to pass that I debunked his handful theory of wishes,

For one week later,

That untrainable dalmatian ran away never to grace my home again –

And with or without dog shit in my hands,

I have been wishing ever since.

Life Ain't Metaphorical

I had to call in late for work because my car was being serviced,

It was no big deal but I also knew that by doing so I would miss the big

Meeting with my boss who hated me with a passion and wanted to fire me -

There was no doubt about it.

My relationship with this woman had become rocky the week before

When she overheard me telling a horribly obscene joke at the office

Christmas party followed by an ill-timed remark about her weight.

She had ceased liking me ever since, and had now reached the point where

She no longer even attempted to conceal her displeasure

At any moment when our paths happened to cross.

These were trying days to be sure, and to make matters worse,

My car had to go into the shop for a repair that I believed

Had to be substantial –

The awful sounds emanating from my vehicle surely indicated

A devastating mechanical issue that would

Require significant funding to correct.

I envisioned drawing all of my savings to pay for the car

As I sat in the waiting room of the service department

Leafing through a two-month old sports magazine

And pondering on what a low point in my life I had reached.

It was then that an oil-stained mechanic walked out holding something

That must have been an important part of my car and

Held it menacingly in front of my face.

I asked, "How bad is it?"

Eggplant Rufus

He smiled and said, "It's fixed."

My shock was significant, and I asked, "How much?"

And he said, "No charge."

My jaw dropped with disbelief –

"Yep, it was just a bolt, no charge," he continued.

"Merry Christmas."

And then I suddenly remembered it was, in fact, Christmas Eve,

And that here I was in a service center where I expected to pay

Thousands of dollars and instead had been given this wonderful kindness

And I thought, "Perhaps my life is coming around."

So I called my boss and I said I was coming right in to work and I wanted to

Sit down with her and discuss our relationship to clear the air so that we

Could have a fresh, productive start heading into the new year.

After all, I thought, it was Christmas Eve, and my day had already started

On a wonderful note with an unexpected kindness from an auto mechanic.

I had dreaded the repair, and my fears were unwarranted.

Within an hour, I sat in the expensive leather chair in front of my boss' desk,

Infused with confidence and watching out the window as the snow

Began to fall on what surely would be a happy Christmas after all.

It took all of five minutes

For that fat fucking bitch

To fire me.

My Cubicle, My Castle

When I was a child I had visions of life

In a future that was filled with jetpacks and liquefied food.

We would all dress in one-piece, tight fitting outfits

With out initials embroidered over our hearts.

It didn't happen,

Not for me,

Not for anyone I know.

The future that I grew up in involves

Spending eight hours a day

Five days a week

In a cubicle castle

With carpeted walls and a large space for a door.

Rather than give us jet packs, food we could eat with a straw,

The powers that be invented the cubicle

And put us all in our very own corporate padded cell.

It is a little zoo of capitalism,

Animals of different departments and breeds

On display

In our little synergistic society.

There are many benefits to this life in a box:

I have unlimited thumb tacks to post photos of my children

Or motivational quotes to keep me awake.

I have a tinted window through which I can view

The complexities of American business life

Eggplant Rufus

Without straining my eyes.

There are manila folders to put papers in

And steel file drawers to put the folders.

 It's all here – all the essentials at my fingertips

In my cubicle castle.

But occasionally, I make a necessary sojourn

Outside of these four walls to find a bathroom

In times of need.

Not jet packs, no food in bottles, no blouses with initials.

Our future turned out to be a soft box without a toilet.

A glass half-empty?

I say half-full,

For one man's box can easily be another man's mansion.

So wipe your feet before you step through the big hole

And into the spacious foyer

Of my cubicle castle.

Goat Knowledge

The goat knows nothing about the fence,

The twisted metal cage around his chunk of the planet.

He does not know that the fence

Cost six dollars more per yard

Because it was union made,

Or that it will last only seven years before rusting through.

He is not aware of the hours of early morning labor

One farmer put himself through

To erect the frame

Or the sacrifices that farmer made

To buy it.

He does not understand metalworking

Or carpentry,

Nor does he recognize

A single tool used in its assembly.

No,

The goat knows nothing about the fence,

Only that it is something he must work his head through

To get to the tall grass

On the other side.

Vietnam

When we were very young boys,

My friend and I believed we lived only a few blocks from Vietnam –

There was a public park near our houses

With heavy foliage and a little stream

That cut through it like the Mekong Delta.

We saw the war on the news every night

And we heard about it at school.

Once, my friend's father took us to a nearby air force base

And we saw a helicopter that had bullet holes in the windshield.

It even smelled bad.

A soldier told us as we held our noses, "that's what Vietnam smells like."

We drove home in his Dad's car,

But when you're too short to see over the dashboard

You don't know where you are,

And being so young and geographically challenged

We believed that the air force base was only a few blocks away

And that the big grassy field around the corner was in reality

Vietnam.

Although everyone tried to tell us the real Vietnam was far away

In some place called South East Asia -

We knew for a fact that we could ride our bikes to it,

And the leafy trees and dense foliage of that park surely hid

Thousands of Viet Cong or North Vietnamese regulars.

We sometimes would walk through the park as a dare to each other –

Eggplant Rufus

Night was especially treacherous.

We never saw any helicopters landing to airlift the wounded or

Fighter jets dropping napalm,

We just assumed that happened

When we were asleep, at school or eating dinner.

Those Viet Cong didn't mess with us for some reason,

Perhaps they were so taken aback by our sheer bravado –

No doubt we were a couple of bad ass little kids

To be walking through a war zone without a weapon.

But you can bet, when we saw a particularly messy battle

On the television news at night,

We kept our asses as far away from the park as possible.

That was the perfect time to head to the basement for a game of ping-pong,

Read a comic book or work on a puzzle.

I'm not sure when that field stopped being Vietnam,

I do recall when we were about twelve years old

It became a pretty great place to play football.

That would make it 1975 over in the real Vietnam and they were airlifting

People off the top of the United States Embassy in Saigon.

For America, the war was over,

And for my friend and I

It was footballs now flying through the air

Instead of grenades and mortar shells.

The war was over

For us too.

Underpants Wisdom

Everyone looks for something to hang their hat on.

You make your way through a lifetime

And you try to pick up a nugget or two

Of information that somehow, someday

You might be remembered for.

You hope that someone's life

Will be enriched because you have walked on this earth.

Here is my nugget for you -

Feel it, absorb it and make it part of your daily life.

Here it is:

Always –

And I mean always –

Keep an extra pair of underpants in your car,

And another pair where you work.

Sooner or later,

You'll need an extra pair of underpants,

And some days,

You might just need

Both.

Mrs. Peters' Peanut Butter

When I was eight,

The best tree house in the neighborhood

Belonged to John Peters.

He was two years older than me,

But if he was by himself on a particular day

He would let me crawl up the ladder nailed to the base

Of the old maple tree in his back yard,

And hang out for an hour or two

In the palatial digs that all the older kids

Would call home every day after school.

He would also crawl down that ladder after an hour or so

And retrieve for me from his kitchen one of his mother's homemade

Peanut butter sandwiches –

The same sandwiches the older kids raved about.

And they were excellent – not filled with Jiff or Skippy –

But a chunkier, sweeter concoction that tasted like his mother

Had poured honey into the bowl while blending the mixture.

One Saturday I went down to the tree house because I knew

That weekends were the best time to have my hour or two inside,

But there was a secret meeting of the Tree House Club

And when I called up asking for John,

They yelled back, "Go away little kid, we're having a meeting."

So I walked away but stopped for a moment at his kitchen window

And peered inside:

Eggplant Rufus

There was John Peters

Meticulously aligning sixteen slices of bread on the kitchen counter

And covering each piece with a spoonful of sugar.

He then retrieved a gallon can of Planters peanuts

And poured them into his mouth.

My jaw dropped open with horror as I watched him chew the nuts,

And subsequently spit them on to the sugarcoated slices of bread.

I walked home in a daze,

Trying to make sense of it all.

It's a kick in the stomach, you see,

When you come to the realization that

You have been eating someone else's chewed-up nuts

Disguised as a peanut butter sandwich.

You look at the world in a very different way

On the walk back to your house that startling day.

Your head spins with a queasy adolescent dilemma

Because you know in your heart that the technique involved

In manufacturing the "homemade peanut butter"

Was unquestionably disturbing,

But spit-out nuts or not,

That tree house was a pretty great place to be

And the sandwiches themselves –

Well they tasted damned fine indeed.

Puzzle for Penance

I have seen a lot of religions in my short stay here on Earth –

Every one of them has their own way of dealing with the mega-issues,

The big screw-ups that we human beings have the uncanny ability

To perform on a regular basis.

For my money, the Catholics have found the easiest way out –

Do something horrible,

Then walk into a dark booth, admit it,

And a Priest tells you to recite a few poems and play with beads.

It seems that all you have to do to pay back on your sin loan

Is repeatedly mumble a few hundred "Hail Mary's"

And shazam - you're clean.

For my money, that just isn't good enough.

One suggestion I could make to the Catholic Church would be to institute

A faith-wide "puzzle policy" for all sins,

Large and small.

If you said the Lord's name in vain, for instance,

The Priest would hand you a 50-piece puzzle of say,

The Empire State Building or one of the maps of the United States

With all the colors and showing the lines that divide the states –

C'mon, you know that's easy.

If you slept with your neighbor's wife,

Well now you are in some serious territory -

And your punishment perhaps a 5,000-piece puzzle

Of nothing but a cloudy sky.

Eggplant Rufus

It would be tough, time-consuming,

And you would sure as hell regret drinking that extra glass of wine

With the woman when you were halfway through that puzzle

And hit that inevitable roadblock where you

Couldn't get another piece in place.

And yep, that's right, your sin is not absolved until you spray that completed

Puzzle with silicone and bring it back to the Priest.

Not only will you have worked off that little tryst in a spiritual sense,

But the Church itself now has an attractive wall hanging for the hallway.

Murder?

That would require a 10,000-piece puzzle of a polar bear in the Antarctic –

A nightmarish task that would have the killer pleading for incarceration,

But the kind of decorative work that when finally finished

Would look absolutely striking in the Church community room.

It's never too late for the Church to change,

To make appropriate variations in its doctrine to align itself

With modern needs.

Who knows, one day soon you might find a Catholic friend

Who cancels a night out on the town with you

Because he has to stay home and finish

A puzzle of two thousand brightly colored gumballs in a glass bowl,

And you will know beyond the shadow of any doubt

That he has been a very bad boy.

Green Curry Epiphany

I am sitting at lunchtime in a tiny Thai restaurant

On Del Mar Avenue in San Clemente, California.

I have ordered a plate of green curried eggplant and shrimp

And am skimming a USA Today waiting for its arrival.

The waitress checks in and pours me a small cup of tea

With a gigantic smile.

She is very nice and quite beautiful,

And I am thinking that a very good looking Thai woman

Is like a little work of art that walks among us.

The curry comes out and it is exquisite,

Creamy and rich with coconut milk loaded with hot pepper and basil.

I am thinking about the business meeting I have to go to in an hour,

But this curry is making that unpleasant task seem like a year away.

The beautiful waitress comes back to my table and asks

"Everything all white?"

By "all white" I assume she is asking if my curry is acceptable

And I nod silently and continue reading my newspaper.

I look up from the paper as she walks away and

I wonder if I were to call my wife right now and talk about this lunch,

How would I describe it?

I would mention the curry and the eggplant and the perfectly cooked rice –

But would I mention the waitress – this tiny Asian work-of-art?

I will never see this waitress again, I won't marry her,

I won't even ask her name.

Eggplant Rufus

But for some reason,

This beautiful woman is now a secret to me and I wonder why.

As I sit eating the green curry I feel something that might be the snap of

Sudden understanding – Why couldn't I tell my wife I had this magnificent

Waitress at the Thai restaurant at lunch today?

Why shouldn't anything that crosses our paths in the course of life

Be available for conversation?

We would all be a lot happier and healthier on many levels,

And most certainly it is quite acceptable to appreciate human beauty

Without having to touch it or own it.

The wonderful waitress returns and takes my credit card.

When she processes the bill,

She brings it to the table and says simply, "Than koo" with a huge

Cheshire cat smile.

I am thinking I should be the one to say "Than koo."

I learned a lot, I think, during this sixty-minute green curry lunch,

And maybe I'm better off or richer somehow because of it.

And I know, as sure as the sun will set over the Pacific

Seven hours from now,

I'll give my wife a call tonight and talk about my meeting in the afternoon,

The beautiful sunset on the California coastline, and the outstanding

Green curry lunch at a little Thai restaurant on Del Mar Avenue.

I think I'll just skip the part about the waitress.

Tubbie in a Tavern

I stopped in Double Jacks Tavern on my way home from work

To pick up some chicken wings for our family dinner.

Double Jacks makes the best wings, and everyone in the family loves them.

While the bartender went back to the kitchen to get my order,

I scanned the bar and saw the usual batch of semi-drunks

And happy hour revelers,

But with one notable exception:

About halfway down the bar, there was a large, pear-shaped green patron

With what appeared to be an antennae pointing up from his head.

He was looking into a bubbling glass of Coors Light the bartender

Had just refilled and placed in front of him.

I watched him a little longer as he took the frosted mug,

Brought it to his lips and drained the contents.

He pushed the empty vessel towards the bartender,

Now returning with a plastic bag containing my chicken wings,

And gave the busy bar employee an irritated look.

He then made an incomprehensible, almost alien, high-pitched noise

That sounded something like the word "more."

The bartender said, "Keep your shirt on."

He took my money for the takeout order and gave me my change.

I stopped him and quietly asked, "is that, by any chance, a Teletubbie?"

"Yep," he replied, "it's Dipsey...comes in here every night."

Wow, I thought, a children's television celebrity in my local bar.

I thought to myself that my two-year old would absolutely shriek

Eggplant Rufus

If I brought home Dipsey's autograph,

So I swiped the bartender's pen and a napkin and stopped at the bar

Right next to him on my way out the tavern door.

"May I have an autograph, please," I asked, "for my two-year old son?"

I placed the napkin on the bartop and put the pen on top of it.

Dipsey ignored me, drinking steadily from his fresh brew.

I pushed the napkin a little closer to him, and with that,

His head whipped around and I found myself staring

Into his bloodshot, alien eyes.

Again, in a high-pitched but this time very discernable voice, he said,

"No fucking autographs."

I grabbed my chicken wings and walked angrily out of the tavern.

Once the door slammed behind me, the cold, fresh air

Of a March Pennsylvania night wrapped around me,

Waking me up to the wonders I had just witnessed.

Holy Shit!

Not one, but two major news flashes.

One – the Teletubbies are real – I saw one!

And two,

They are not nearly as friendly

As they appear on television.

Heaven

So many times I think

There isn't much out there

But planets and space.

After all,

We flew to the moon

And couldn't find Heaven.

But what if it's actually out there somewhere,

Maybe past the last known planet,

Or in the Sun.

But the Sun would probably be Hell anyway

And who wants to spend time with Hitler and Ted Bundy -

Is that any kind of acceptable way to spend eternity?

And if Heaven were out past where Pluto used to be,

Even the most gentle and agreeable soul

Would grumble about spending their afterlife shivering

In complete darkness -

Does that seem like the kind of eternal reward

Any of us expected

For being good boys and girls all our lives?

My friend said his goal in life was to make a few people laugh

And somehow make it to Heaven –

A kind of loophole or technicality that says,

"Ok, I didn't follow the rules,

But I made a few people happy along the way."

Eggplant Rufus

Maybe that's one way of getting into Heaven,

Or maybe

One could build an enormous rocket ship with external fuel tanks

The size of Delaware

To shoot that vehicle into the far end of the universe

And crash that party where the good souls congregate.

Then again, Maybe not a rocket ship

Or good deeds or

Making a few people laugh –

Maybe none of those are necessary,

Because I am in Heaven right now

On the sofa in my living room

Where I sit with my feet on a coffee table

While I hold a sleeping

Six-month old baby boy.

To get to Heaven this day,

I didn't need a rocket ship,

Just a comfortable couch to sit on and a television set

To put in front of it

And a little boy

To sleep in my arms.

Boogers

I live in fear of boogers,

These thoughtless clumps of matter in my nostrils.

I have seen too many fine people

Needlessly degraded and berated

For having even the tip of a booger exposed.

At crowded gatherings I touch my face from time to time

To assure myself

That no booger made a dash for freedom

And was lodged on my upper lip.

Why so nomadic, these boogers?

Is there something so terribly wrong with the snug, warm and

Cozy confines of my nasal cavity?

Not a penthouse, perhaps,

But not a Devil's Island either to inspire such a ceaseless

Preoccupation with escape.

I sometimes think of boogers

As cruel, vile little creatures with no sense of responsibility,

Leaving home without a thought for their loved ones.

Perhaps they too live in constant turmoil and fear

Always watchful and waiting

For the next bad cold and the inevitable

Flood from my sinuses.

And, perhaps,

They are the most accurate indicators of my health –

Eggplant Rufus

A kind of coal miner's canary for my state of being.

If I see a dozen or so boogers bail out,

It is surely a sign of greater troubles ahead.

I live with them, these parasites,

And take them with me everywhere I go.

To my senior prom in high school

I brought at least eleven boogers,

Although three rudely skydived to get a look at my date.

A full fourteen boogers

Accepted my diploma with me at college

And at a Governor's Ball one politically ambitious booger lodged himself

On the lapel of my tuxedo to say a few words to the state's highest official.

I suppose, therefore, though I fear them,

I must respect and accept them

And in their honor always take horrified offense

To those godless cannibals who mercilessly

Eat their boogers.

Frank's New Attitude

Frank was listless and

Unenthralled with life.

The world thought him a marshmallow –

A sniveling, twig-legged stick drawing sitting on a beach towel

With a bully forever kicking sand in his face.

One day Frank had finally had enough

And decided to make a change.

First, he spent fourteen hundred dollars on the latest contraption

Sold to develop a body-builder's physique.

For another two hundred dollars,

He invested in recorded seminars of several famous

Motivational speakers

Where he learned about focus, clarity and staying on task.

He read several books from respected psychologists

To learn to be sensitive and caring,

All the while pulling his personal gym from under his bed

Each morning and day-by-day growing in

Physical strength and personal confidence.

He bought a shiny Jaguar, the latest model,

With a ragtop convertible roof

And charged a brand new wardrobe

On his newly acquired gold and platinum credit cards

And paid the bills off promptly at the end of the month.

Finally, after all of these improvements,

Eggplant Rufus

He met the woman of his dreams

And they quickly fell in love.

She was overwhelmed with his sense of caring,

His nurturing soul,

His tasteful style of dress

And his rock-hard physique.

They flew to a church in the Midwest where he paid for

Her entire family to watch their marriage,

Then the newlyweds jetted off to the Bahamas

For a honeymoon they could cherish for the rest of their lives.

After they made love on the beach,

They walked hand-in-hand to a little bistro with a beautiful deck

Overlooking the sparkling blue water of the Caribbean

And toasted each other with mimosas.

For an appetizer, Frank ordered conch,

A local delicacy he had read about in an epicurean magazine,

And took a forkful as he looked into the eyes of his new wife.

At that moment,

Microscopic parasites infesting the poorly cooked seafood

Swam straight to his brain and touched a nerve center which

Immediately stopped his heart -

Killing him right there at the table.

Goes to show you, doesn't it?

You just can't have everything.

Yard Balls

They sit on concrete cylinders in American front yards,

Gleaming tributes to the permanency of ownership

And "every man's home is his castle."

They are yard balls

And I describe them as tributes because

Otherwise there could be no explanation

As to how or why these gleaming metallic spheres

Appeared on this planet.

They are all sizes and colors -

Red, yellow, green, blue -

And you could pay a hundred bucks for one

If you wanted to.

Away from their bases they roll quite nicely

And once, I confess, I sent one winging down a suburban back street

For no good reason at all.

But once, I also admit,

The sun shone just right off a yard ball on the Maryland coast

And I swear I saw Heaven

Or at least a neat looking cloud.

So they aren't all bad,

These yard balls.

They are like so many of us:

Gleaming on pedestals,

Without purpose

And owned by someone else.

Brains on Tiananmen Square

If Bob Hope were there he would have said

"Tanks for the memories,"

But Bob wasn't there,

In fact

There was very little hope at all,

Just blood, sweat and brains on Tiananmen Square.

I saw a photograph of a Chinese student

Squashed

With his brains two feet behind him.

Those same brains that only an hour before

Thought democracy was a pretty good idea

Probably had a different opinion now.

Nontheless,

Everyone who saw the scene

No doubt believed him a hero in the struggle

Against the government.

It's funny the way that works sometimes,

When the masses gather strength and unity from heroic death.

But if you would ask those brains

Baking on the Beijing concrete,

They would tell you

They would much prefer to be in a field behind an ox

And kissing Mao's red Bible

As long as they were still attached to the rest of their body.

Eggplant Rufus

Back in 1989,

It was like Woodstock in China for a month or so,

And for a week like My Lai.

When it was over,

No one knew how many brains had spilled

And even the President of the United States

Got a busy signal.

But I know for certain that one Chinese student

Met his new professor

And learned that even democracy,

Good intentions and the highest ideals

Can't keep a set of brains in your head

When a twelve-ton tank wants to go downtown

And you are in the way.

Most Beautiful Woman

I am sitting at a restaurant on a rainy afternoon.

The lunch crowd pours through the doors,

And the place is soon filled with kids, parents and businesspeople.

I walk to the salad bar and grab a seat nearby

Reading the latest news in a USA Today.

A trio of kids with their soccer uniforms on passes by and make their way

To the salad bar to build their lunch.

I give them a passing glance,

And then notice a woman filling her plate in front of them.

She is perhaps thirty years old,

Perfectly proportioned and working her way through the salad bar

With a kind of natural grace.

I hear the three boys now standing directly next to her

Begin to giggle and point,

And they say, "Gross lady."

She turns to them and smiles and continues making her salad,

And as she acknowledges them,

I notice that all the skin on her face has been burned off

And a large part of her nose is missing.

One of the boys drops his plate when she looks at him

And the three of them run back to their

Perfectly attired soccer mom chaperone.

I turn back to the woman in time to see her put dressing on her greens

And return to her seat on the other side of the salad bar.

Eggplant Rufus

She has a magazine she is reading as she dines alone,

And looks up for a moment when the boys return with several more

Soccer friends who sneak up to catch a glimpse of her.

She smiles again and nods,

And the boys run back to their tables.

Their mother scolds them slightly and implores them to sit

While trying to sneak her own glance at the object of their merriment.

But the woman dining alone

Has already forgiven and forgotten the boys

And continues reading her magazine.

This is not the first nor will it be the last

Scene of its kind in her life.

As I look on I feel a little sorry for myself

Because I know every woman I meet from this day on

Will never measure up –

I have already seen the most beautiful woman in the world.

Drink Restoration

Baby, you will never know

That in the time

It took you to walk away from me at the bar

To go to the ladies room,

I ordered the same drink

I was drinking when you left

And downed the new one completely,

Leaving my existing drink in the same state

That it was when you left.

When you returned,

It appeared as if

Nothing

Had changed at all.

When you sat down,

We began a conversation about honesty

In our relationship

And how we are different than all the other couples

Because we can tell each other

Everything.

I agreed with a smile and kissed you

Softly on the lips,

Then took a sip from my cocktail

Waiting patiently

For your next trip to the bathroom.

Spider on a White Wall

It is midnight and I am sitting at my desk

In the basement of my house.

There is a blank open document on my computer

And I want to write a poem

About two old men who get themselves killed

While stealing a car in the parking lot

Of the nursing home where they reside.

It is a story that has everything - irony, action, drama, violence -

And even has a sad-but-true ending

In which the two nursing home residents

And would-be car thieves drive off a bridge while pursued by a dozen cops.

I want to call it "Joy Ride."

I look from the computer screen to the equally blank

White painted concrete wall

In front of me.

The wall is blank and white on purpose.

I can see the world as I want it to be when I look at that wall,

And I can project little films on it in my mind

And write down what I see.

Tonight I am ready to start the film about the elderly auto theft,

But instead I see only you,

Bastard ugly spider staring at me motionless

On my wall of dreams.

Aren't you even the slightest bit aware that I am vastly larger than you

Eggplant Rufus

And would prefer at this moment that you were dead?

Why don't you move?

What are you thinking about?

And most importantly, what is there within an arm's length of my desk

That I can use to squash your brains out?

There is a paperback novel only inches from my grasp and I lunge for it.

You watch me make the move,

Still stoic, unmoving,

Bastard little eight-legged martyr -

Put up your dukes!

But no... you prefer to sit and look at me.

Helpless.

I count to ten - giving you an intentional and I think very fair head start.

You refuse to take me up on the offer so I put on my

Head-of-the-planet homo sapien face

And crush you with a single blow.

Our encounter on this earth is over midnight spider,

But in the end,

You are the winner now mangled on my snow-white wall.

From now until your dried remains flake and fall to the ground,

All the movies I run on that wall will have spider guts on them,

And tonight

When I want to write about two old men in a stolen car,

I have to write

About you.

Cold Meat Loaf Sandwiches

While driving aimlessly through the fields and green

Of America's agricultural heartland

I happened to pass a well-constructed red barn

With the words "Jesus May Come Tomorrow"

Painted across the side of the structure

Between the second and third floors.

I immediately began to imagine the family within that farmhouse,

And their meticulous preparations for dinner,

With the mother nervously checking and re-checking

The meat loaf in the oven

And the children dressed in their Sunday best frocks

And the father pulling and re-pulling at his bow tie

And fussing with his moustache

In front of the mirror in the master bedroom

And the family waiting in the living room

With the fire crackling and the conversation stopping and starting

And building and falling off until finally,

There is no conversation at all

And the youngest and most innocent of the clan asks,

"Mommy, can we eat the meat loaf now?"

The mother looks at the father who looks at his watch one more time

And nods his agreement

Before taking off his dinner jacket and loosening his bow tie.

Mother takes the meat loaf from the oven –

Eggplant Rufus

Now cold and crusted –

While the father gingerly and carefully removes the extra plate

From the dining room table.

The mother walks up to the father's side and puts her arm around

His waist and gives him a kiss on the cheek

While the children remove a loaf of bread from the pantry

And begin cutting up the chilled meat loaf for sandwiches.

She squeezes her husband again for good measure,

And with the kind of understanding that only a woman

Who loves her man despite his insanity can muster,

Whispers in his ear,

"Don't worry honey,

Jesus may come

Tomorrow."

Tight Game

Buddha ate his own excrement in the desert

And some folks find that admirable.

Nonetheless,

I still think Charles Lindbergh was cooler,

Patton had more balls

And Einstein looked better in a leather jacket.

But none of them to my knowledge

Ate their own shit,

So in that department it's

One-zip,

Buddha.

One Hundred Years Hence

I received a coffee mug as a gift today

With a motivational inscription reminding me

That one hundred years from now

The only thing that will really matter

Will be the influence I had

On a child.

The message told me that it would not matter

What kind of car I drove,

How much money I had in the bank

Or what designers I wore.

All that mattered, it concluded,

Was how much light I brought into a child's life.

I took it to heart

And when my boys came home from school,

I hugged then both warmly

And told them how much I loved them

And how much I believed in them.

After the exchange,

They ran upstairs to play a videogame.

I had intended to spend a sizeable portion of the evening

Balancing my checkbook

And paying bills for such obligations as

Car payments, mortgages, utilities and credit cards –

But since none of that will mean shit

Eggplant Rufus

In one hundred years,

And having already done my part with the children,

I decided to drive to the closest tavern

For happy hour.

As I sat at the bar,

I felt satisfied and content

Because of the mug and its wisdom.

Sure, my life is essentially meaningless,

But what the hell – at least now I know it.

But I have accomplished my primary function today:

My children,

Though now sitting at home alone while I hurriedly guzzle

Half-price liquor,

Were enlightened this day by my unsolicited nurturing

And thus, a century from this very afternoon,

Their life will have been enhanced by

By my existence.

As I ordered another drink, however,

That moderate sense of fulfillment was eradicated

By a single, speculative thought:

What if, somewhere along the way during the next

One hundred years,

My children receive as a gift

The same damned mug?

Funeral Pies

At a bar in the anthracite coal region of Pennsylvania,

A fellow named Carl is telling me over Yuengling Lagers

About raisin and prune

Funeral pies.

In this area it seems a tradition to bake pies

Of raisin and prune

For the family of the recently deceased.

On a Sunday morning, for instance, when walking to the store for the paper

Or to the church for a weekly service,

If one should catch the unmistakable aroma of raisin and prune

Wafting in the wind,

Then it was a good bet the little town's census had been reduced by one.

And beyond those pies, it was also a tradition

To display the lifeless body on a sofa in the living room

For a day or so after passing,

And neighbors and friends

Would gather in the kitchen for cocktails, shared memories

And a plateful of pie.

At night,

The children of the house would peer through the darkness

And clutch their beds with every sound

From downstairs

For fear that the body had sprung from the couch

For a mouthful of raisin and prune pie

Eggplant Rufus

Or a gin and tonic.

There is no doubt that a lot of youthful sleep

Has been lost on windy nights

With a corpse on the sofa.

But in the morning,

Just like Christmas,

The present remained in the living room

And Santa's bag was stuffed

With funeral pies.

In Debt

I owe you money.

It is a simple thing,

The way it happened.

I was out of money,

You offered me some

And I took it.

Now you want it back

And when I see you,

I think about how your life

Must have been diminished

By the twenty dollars

You gave to me,

How many opportunities you are missing

Because I am holding out,

And I think how frail a life it must be

For twenty dollars

To make such a difference.

Today I don't even recall

What that twenty dollars was for -

I only know that as I stand here

My pocket is filled with tens, twenties and fifties

And you are standing in front of me

With your hand

Outstretched.

Eggplant Rufus

How does it feel, I wonder,

To crave the return of those

Twenty American dollars and to know

Without a doubt

That my jeans contain hundreds

Of crisp new pieces of currency

Only twenty of which

Would bring your life back to the order it enjoyed

Before our original encounter?

How does it feel

To know even further and beyond the shadow

Of any reasonable doubt

That I have no intention

Of ever

Paying you back?

Esther's Hooters

Esther's hooters are big and bulky,

"We should have them bronzed,"

Her husband Herbert would say at parties.

They're just that damned big.

She's fifty-three now and has lived with these monstrosities

For better than thirty-five years.

Herbert's lived with them for twenty-one -

Since the day they met at a drag race in Madison, Wisconsin.

She loved him right away

Because they dated a full three times before he said

"Let me grab a hold of just one of them titties."

Their mobile home is a double-wide with a new plastic skirt

Around the bottom and a foot-high plastic picket fence enclosing a yard

Big enough for a half-dozen chaise lounges and a barbeque grill.

Herbert has been building a concrete barbeque pit for two years

And hopes to have it done for the summer,

When his buddies come over on weekends to watch NASCAR,

Drink a few beers and stare at Esther's hooters as she sunbathes

On a blue and white lounge chair at the front of the trailer.

Her body isn't what it used to be with her thighs blowing up

And the paunch at her waist growing with each passing year,

But those hooters,

They still stand at attention like two space shuttles

On twin launch pads at Cape Canaveral.

Eggplant Rufus

Herbert loves those hooters and he loves Esther,

Their life support system.

He tells the story almost every day about the time Esther

Walked out of the shower

Into the bedroom where he was running the air conditioning full blast.

"Almost poked my damn eyes out!" he says with a snort

And always mischievously elbows the listener.

If you corner him at a party, Herbert will gladly tell you about the time he

Took his wife to the Daytona 500 and he will swear on a stack of Bibles

That Richard Petty slowed down twice during the race

To get a closer look at Esther's luggage.

"He lost that race, you know," Herbert adds proudly.

Ask Esther about those hooters and she'll tell you

"Some people are just blessed, I don't know."

But hooters like that, well that's more than a blessing.

Men have shopped a lot longer in Wal-Mart than they wanted to

Just to get a glimpse of them, but only one man has a season ticket.

And as night descends on this peaceful trailer park,

Herbert closes his eyes And gives thanks to God for his health,

For NASCAR in general and Jeff Gordon in particular,

And most of all, he thanks the Good Lord almighty

For Esther's hooters.

Yohnee Bopping

In Lancaster, Pennsylvania,

The natives live side-by-side with the Amish, a sect of Dutch and

German descendent farmers who cling to the past with relentless tenacity.

They drive in horse and buggy carriages and dress in black

And denounce electricity.

For the younger Amish, bicycles are the most common form of locomotion

Even when they reach an age when most teenagers

Are begging for the car keys.

It is all a very peaceful scene and profitable as a tourist attraction –

The modern world intermingling with the culture of a bygone age.

But below the surface of what appears a harmonious relationship,

You might find a sub current of chaos.

A college friend named Bill was born in a tiny town not far from

The flocks of Amish.

I always liked Bill, a brawny football player who was asked to leave college

After two years for a variety of violations – but before he left he told me

A few stories that changed my life – just like this one.

Bill and his friends, when younger and in high school, referred to those kind,

Gentle Amish as "Yohnees" and among his friends they developed

A ritual on Friday evenings that is performed nowhere else.

They would gather at a local McDonalds in several cars and begin a drive

Through the back roads of Lancaster County –

Each car possessing a broom stick with a boxing glove tied to the end of it

And one person in the back seat who was in control of it.

Eggplant Rufus

When they happened upon a "Yohnee" riding innocently on his bicycle,

They would extend the broom stick out an open car window

And knock the Amishman off the bike.

Hence, "Yohnee Bopping."

It is without a doubt a dangerous occupation – especially for the Yohnee.

But Bill told me with a big grin that the thrill of watching a black-clad

Freshly-bopped Amish boy careen into a drainage ditch

Was without measure.

He told me tales of his best nights in which dozens of Yohnees

Were left sprawled in shoulders, embankments and guard rail.

At the end of each evening, the group would meet back at McDonalds

And disclose how many Amish had been separated from their bikes

By each car – the winner would have their fast food paid for by the losers.

I tell you this story not to alarm you or lower your opinion of your fellow man

And the mayhem he may be capable of creating – instead it is a

Simple warning that nothing in this world

Is as serene as it may look on the surface.

Remember this tale the next time you pass an Amish farm and you see

The well-manicured fields with oxen pulling century-old tillers manned by

Bearded Amish farmers – and remember it when you're tempted to say,

"Now isn't that lovely – they have no modern conveniences

Yet they are as happy as we!"

Remember that somewhere across town,

A young man is tightening the boxing glove at the end of a broom stick,

Waiting for nightfall.

Condoms

My friend Timothy said that the world was so out of hand

That in hotel rooms, they should put a condom

In addition to the Gideon's Bible

In the drawer by the bed.

The only dilemma of course is which to reach for first.

They should probably put condoms in those plastic-sealed

Knife, fork and napkin packs at Kentucky Fried Chicken

Instead of handi-wipes,

And every glove compartment of every new car sold

Should contain at least a three-pack of condoms

With directions on how to use them.

After all, have you seen people drive?

At a college Halloween party,

A friend of mine put a white trash bag over his head

And went dressed as a condom.

After the party, we all went to an all-night diner downtown and the waitress

Immediately looked at his costume as we ordered and said,

"And what will Mr. Trash bag have to eat?"

"He's not a trash bag, lady," I said, "he's a walking prophylactic."

She screamed as if seeing a ghost

And dashed into the kitchen to talk to the manager.

They ended up telling us to leave that night,

That no one dressed like a rubber could eat in a public place,

But for half-a-buck,

Eggplant Rufus

You could walk into the men's room of that same diner

And buy various brightly colored condoms for sale

Through a vending machine

Nailed to the wall.

So here I am again,

Confronted with another of life's great hypocrisies

In the least likely of places,

And here it is:

For a couple of quarters you can buy a condom,

Return to your booth and enjoy your ham and eggs,

But if you happen to be dressed as one

You might as well not even pick up a menu.

Twenty Thousand Dead Chicks

It was a Friday morning and poised for a sunny June weekend

I opened the newspaper

To kick-off the final day of the working week.

Inside, a tragedy of almost unheard of dimensions confronted me.

Buried on page seven of the local section

Was the sorrowful account of a traffic mishap on routes eleven and fifteen

In which a tractor-trailer turned on its side

Sending 20,000 day-old chicks spilling across the interstate

Like fluffy, yellow marbles.

The article happily reported that the driver was uninjured

Because he wore his seat belt.

Apparently, he did not care enough to provide 20,000 tiny belts

For his passengers.

It was a scene one could imagine vividly –

The ambulances, the fire trucks,

The coroner pronouncing the deaths

Of 20,000 day-old chicks.

Twenty thousand tiny green blankets pulled over the beaks of

Twenty thousand victims,

And 20,000 chalk outlines on the concrete.

And for the drivers who followed on this road of carnage,

One can only imagine the horror, the unspeakable tragedy,

And uncontrollable hydroplaning

On the mashed remains

Eggplant Rufus

Of 20,000 future drumsticks and thighs.

I hope he can't sleep tonight,

That truck driver,

Haunted by the incessant peeping

Of 20,000 day-old

Ghosts

Who never saw a twenty-fifth hour

On routes eleven and fifteen.

Amanda Behind Glass

Amanda wants to be an attorney

And is in her third year at George Washington University.

She studies every evening until the small hours of the morning

While working behind the glass

At Jo Jo's Flesh-O-Rama on 18th Street

In the nation's capitol.

Corporate law is a bitch, she has to admit,

And knuckles down memorizing the fine print for an upcoming exam

Until the buzzer sounds and the corrugated steel door lifts

To reveal three sailors on the other side of the glass.

"Show us your stuff," they say,

And for exactly three minutes she bends and rolls and dips

Until the time limit bell sounds and the steel curtain

Drops to the floor.

Amanda picks up her textbook again

And reviews her Latin while sitting on the cold steel stool.

"Oh this fiduciary nonsense!" she gasps,

Until the door again rises to reveal six Japanese businessmen.

She takes a quick scan of her glossary for "Amicus Curiae"

While fulfilling the businessmen's request of

Pushing her buttocks against the six-inch thick plexiglass.

They run their hands against the glass as if grabbing at her exposed skin

While she attempts to remember

A precedent set in the Rhode Island Supreme Court in 1977.

Eggplant Rufus

Amanda is a good student, you see, with a fine memory

And was B-plus student

Until that fateful day when the Dean of the law school

Walked into Jo Jo's with a roll of quarters.

Her grade point average soared significantly as a result.

She dreams of graduation and her own office

Without glass or steel or buzzers,

Rather oak and leather with shelves of books

And her own paralegal.

But for now,

The dream each time is extinguished

By the gentle tinkling of American coins

And the grating sound

Of corrugated steel.

Four Dimes in Your Pocket

Oh my friend,

One piece of advice I happily share with you

Is to carry four dimes in your right pants pocket

Every night that you head out to a tavern

Or in any situation where alcohol might pass through your lips.

I have just abandoned you at the bar tonight

After we had dinner earlier and took a cab back to our hotel.

On the taxi ride home,

You were laughing,

Told a few jokes,

And you were generally an absolute

Joy

To be around.

You had four glasses of red wine with dinner

And it had put you in just the right frame of mind

For an enjoyable evening.

When we returned to the hotel

It seemed perfectly reasonable to have a single nightcap

That would represent the appropriate closure

To our evening together.

It was, however, your fifth drink of the night

And instantly transformed you into a raging asshole.

You spewed out anger, negativity and a

Wicked sense of arrogance I never knew you possessed.

Eggplant Rufus

After forty-five minutes,

I pretended my cell phone was ringing and ran as fast as I could

To my room to get away from you.

So here now sitting on my hotel bed,

I write these words and offer this advice:

Carry the four dimes in your right pocket,

And with each drink you consume,

Transfer one dime to your left.

When you find that you have forty cents

In that left pocket,

Stop drinking immediately

This exercise will prevent the startling transformation that turns a

Pleasant evening into a session of suffering.

Those forty cents will keep the monster within,

The asshole will remain in its cage.

And if you need the four dimes to make it happen,

For God's sake,

Just ask –

I always have four for myself

Anyway.

Infected Butt

Every time it rained, the little park up the street from where I grew up
Would flood covering the grass and basketball court with six inches
Of water.
When you're a seven-year-old kid,
You didn't worry about the drainage issues that caused the flooding,
You just yelled "yahoo" and ran to the park when the skies opened up.
One day there were a dozen second-graders at the park
Splashing and surfing on the deluge,
And I was one of them.
I had just used four firecrackers to blow up a plastic model of the
USS Missouri that I had painstakingly assembled the previous weekend.
One of our cohorts approached us with a stick that had a golf ball-sized
Chunk of mud and grass hanging from the end of it.
We thought this dude was cracked to begin with, but now he was asking for
A dollar from every one of us, and in exchange for that payment
He would Insert that muddy stick up his ass.
Being kids out in the rain, none of us had money
But he assured us he would collect the next day at school.
And so it was that he then pulled his pants down,
And while we hid behind each other to keep from looking at the act,
This childhood chum shoved that muddy stick into his butt.
When he pulled it out,
There was nothing on the end of it – the grassy concoction that had earlier
Clung to the tip of the stick was now lodged inside him somewhere.

Eggplant Rufus

The next day we all came to school with a dollar

But he wasn't there to collect his payment for the deed.

He had spent the night in the emergency room and would not come back

To school for three months having contracted some near deadly infection

From the painful performance that afternoon

At our flooded neighborhood park.

And when he finally did return to our classroom,

He did not receive our money but rather a nickname -

"Infected butt" -

Which he would retain until his parents moved away two years later.

There is a lot to be learned from this tale,

And certainly part of this knowledge is some simple wisdom

Of how cruel children can be to each other.

But to me, the lessons learned are more practical and specific:

First, if you are going to put a stick up your butt for money,

Then collect that money before performing the deed as you will

Most assuredly spend a considerable amount of time recovering from

Whatever infection you acquire in the process.

And probably more importantly, If you're even considering putting a

Muddy stick up your ass for money - just forget the whole idea.

You won't earn a lot of money, you won't gain fame,

You'll only most likely acquire a nickname you won't like

And within a couple of years

You'll have to move away.

Witness Protection Program

I would like to be in the witness protection program.

Is there some way

I can sign up?

I don't have any pertinent information that I can offer up

To put anyone away

But for the right offer

I could plagiarize the plot of a Coppola or Scorcese movie

And create a perfectly believable scenario

Of anyone's involvement in nearly any crime.

And not only am I well-versed in classic theatrical organized crime drama,

I additionally have near-photographic recollection

Of every Sopranos episode,

Knowledge that might come in handy for the off-the-cuff remarks

Necessary during cross-examination.

My resume, therefore, is airtight.

In exchange for this performance I request only the usual beige

Two-bedroom home in a middle-class suburban neighborhood

With the paper delivered daily including Sundays.

I would also, of course, need a new name –

Preferably something mysterious and foreign.

A new identity would additionally be in order,

And here I am flexible as long as my government-invented profession

Involves international espionage or some kind of important

Medical research that is secretly conducted in my fully outfitted

Eggplant Rufus

Basement laboratory.

For these simple demands,

The government can have any habitual evil-doer locked up for good,

And I would feel a gratifying sense of public service

While picking up my newspaper in the driveway

And chatting with my new neighbors on the progress of the life saving

Experiments that are underway

In the bowels of my two-bedroom rancher.

So please give me a call,

I am ready for the witness protection program

And all the anonymity it can provide –

You can find me easily in the telephone book,

At least, that is,

For now.

Think Tank

It seems incomprehensible to me that no great literature

Has confronted the most natural ritual of humanity.

It has been advanced that man's greatest accomplishment

Is civilization,

But what of these whimsical daily accomplishments

We amateur magicians perform in the privacy

Of our own bathrooms?

What can Houdini have accomplished compared to our ability

To turn a four-course Italian dinner

Into a few tiny packages that could fit in a cigar box?

And the toilet is too often ignored in historical analysis as well –

How many of Kennedy's decisions during the 1961 Missile Crisis

Were made while dispensing with an Oval Office

Late night dinner?

Is it too much to assume that at least a portion

Of Abe Lincoln's Gettysburg Address

Was composed on the john on those rickety tracks to Gettysburg?

Or perhaps two years later,

Was General Lee's decision to surrender affirmed in his mind

While saying goodbye to a southern grits casserole

In an Appomattox outhouse?

I read once that medical science could,

One day in the future and by some means well beyond understanding,

Eliminate the need for man to use the toilet at all -

Eggplant Rufus

Instead converting waste into a substance resembling perspiration

That we would simply secrete through our pores

During the course of the day.

If this should ever become a reality,

I hope the conversion is voluntary –

I still have a few important decisions to make in my life

And I know where I want to make them.

Mansions of Rhode Island

I am touring the mansions of Newport, Rhode Island –

A majestic row of opulence overlooking the ocean.

They were called "summer cottages" by their owners

And are so large they have names

Like "The Breakers," "The Elms," "Marble House," and "Rosecliff."

They are splendid displays of high-Victorian architecture

And you need a map to navigate the endless ballrooms, libraries

And staff quarters.

The Vanderbilts built "The Breakers" – a 70-room Italian-style palazzo

And Nevada silver heiress Theresa Fair Oelrichs

Had "Rosecliff" built in the image of the Grand Trianon,

The opulent retreat of the French kings at Versailles.

She had wonderful parties at her chateau,

Even hosting a gig visited by the great Harry Houdini.

Edwin Julius Berwind made his fortune in the Pennsylvania coal industry

And took his cash to Rhode Island to build "The Elms,"

While William Shepherd Wetmore took his earnings

And constructed a monstrosity called "Chateau-Sur-Mer"

Along the row of mansions.

The tour guides point out the real gold used in the paint,

The superior molding,

The tons of marble and stone used in construction.

They tell tales of grandiose events held within the walls of the mansions,

And of mysterious love triangles and family squabbles.

Eggplant Rufus

I have seen five mansions now with a few more to go,

And I have already seen enough.

I see the rest of the tour group filing around the corner and

Disappear in the rear view mirror of my mid-sized sedan.

I suppose there are a lot of feelings you can take home as a souvenir

From your tour of the mansions of Rhode Island –

And one of them might be a cocktail of awe with a dash

Of regret regarding the things you don't have in life.

But sitting here drinking a cup of espresso at a tiny coffee shop

A few blocks from where those summer cottages overlook the Atlantic,

I am struck with the notion that despite differences

In architecture, interior layout and furnishings,

All of those oversized homes have one thing in common –

All of their original occupants

Are dead as doornails.

And I am not.

Hell, I'll trade that for a fucking mansion

Any day of the week.

By the Side of the Road

You never know what you will find

By the side of the road.

That is what one Nevada State Trooper found one

Evening when he came upon a four-year old Mexican girl

Who was holding tightly to a speed limit sign.

He was the first on the scene of an accident,

And on the other side of the highway from where the girl sat,

A van was ablaze having driven off the road

And into a barrier.

The trooper called for assistance,

And began to comfort the little girl

Who was calm despite the situation.

He asked for information,

And she said there was a loud crash and the car

Stopped violently and then there was smoke

Followed by flames she could see

In the front of the car.

She had struggled with her child seat and belt trying in a panic

To free herself.

At the height of her predicament,

Her mother and father calmly explained to her

How to unfasten the belt,

And once she had removed the restraint,

Told her to open the door of the car.

They then walked her hand-in-hand across the highway

And told her to hold on to the

Speed limit sign until help arrived.

"Where are they now?" the trooper asked.

The child shrugged and said simply, "They disappeared."

The trooper looked around the area and saw no one.

When the fire department arrived and put out the blaze,

They found both the mother and father

Possibly killed by the impact of the collision

And then burned completely

While still strapped into their seat belts.

The trooper was holding the little girl when the Fire Chief

Told him the news.

But the trooper already knew, or had a suspicion.

He had been on this job long enough to understand

That you never know

What you will find

On this stretch of desert highway –

Sometimes a little girl who survived a car accident,

Sometimes a burning van

And sometimes a glimpse into eternity,

All of which were waiting for him on this star-filled autumn night

By the side of the road.

Autumn in New York

I was slurping up the oil at the bottom of a plate

Of anchovies and pimento at Pete's Tavern

That Saturday lunchtime

In October.

The food was so wonderful I hardly noticed the woman

Three seats down from me at the bar.

She was watching me, amazed, as I swallowed the salty little fish

And soaked red peppers.

"How can you eat that?" she asked with a smile.

The sunlight from outside danced off her grin and twinkled in her eye

And I knew something special had just occurred.

We shared a couple of beers and talked about nothing but somehow

Sitting there and saying nothing was the greatest thing I could have done.

She suggested a cab ride to South Street Seaport so we headed out of the

Tavern and within minutes were walking among the harbor shops

And restaurants,

Past a young artist who had painted herself green

And stood atop a milk crate holding a paper mache torch

As a living Statue of Liberty.

We dropped a dollar into her traditional starving artist coffee can

Before heading into an old sailor's bar for a pint of Guinness.

Where the brown foam from the beer clung to her upper lip

Like an Irish moustache and we

Giggled like children.

Eggplant Rufus

Outside, the late afternoon crowd hustled back and forth
As the autumn sun began to set.
She asked if she could make dinner for the two of us at her apartment,
And I replied, "yes" as if I had waited for that question my entire life.
She held my hand in the cab ride uptown and I felt like
Telling her my life story.
In my mind I ran scenarios - I will marry her tomorrow, I began to imagine,
And we will ride a horse and buggy through Central Park
Sipping champagne and making plans for the rest of our lives.
Our taxi stopped in front of an old brownstone and I paid the driver.
The smell of chestnuts roasting hit both of us as we emerged from the cab
And she smiled with delight, "The first chestnuts of the year!"
"Then we must have them," I said and handed her a fifty dollar bill,
"Run around the corner and buy some - buy enough for the whole city!"
I watched as she blew me a kiss and danced around the corner
To where the chestnut smoke curled into the sky.
I am in love, I thought to myself, I am in love like I have never
Felt before in my life and it happened on a beautiful autumn day
In the city that never sleeps.
I waited another twenty minutes for her to return with the chestnuts
And realized with complete certainty that
I would never see that thieving slut again.

Chickens on the Beach

At a McDonald's in Salisbury, Maryland,

You can choose to sit on the outdoor patio and eat your Big Macs

And Happy Meals and McChickens

Directly across the street from the Perdue chicken factory.

During your meal you will be treated to a gentle

Snowstorm

Of feathers that float down and around you

From the tens of thousands of chickens being killed and processed

For human food inside the plant.

My family would stop at this McDonald's for dinner

Every year while driving to Ocean City for a long weekend vacation.

While I chewed my cheeseburger I always thought about

Those bulging chicken eyes

When the eighteen-wheel truck carrying them in countless cages

Took a right turn into the factory instead of staying on the highway

Which leads to ocean.

They learned quite suddenly at that moment

That they were not going to the shore for a weekend away

From the farm,

But instead were at the short-end of the countdown to the

Unceremonious end of their existences.

So if you ever wonder why you never see chickens sunbathing

On the hot sands of Ocean City,

Or walking the boardwalk eating french fries

Eggplant Rufus

Or sneaking into bars with fake ID's,

Remember that route 50 runs straight through Salisbury

And to the Perdue factory

Across the street from McDonalds.

Tight Blue Dresses

Let me tell you about what is going on here one day in June of 1987

On this blue little ball called Earth.

In China, the students want democracy

And the head honcho of the country

Has prostate cancer but still orders the army

To squash demonstrations for freedom

And there is no clear idea of what the future will bring.

In Iran, the Ayatollah just bought the farm and hoards of grieving Muslims

Tore at his shroud with such intensity that his wrinkled corpse

Fell to the Persian dirt.

A pipeline exploded in the Ural Mountains

And one thousand unfortunate Russians were incinerated in two trains

That chose that moment to pass by.

We just found out that fifty nuclear warheads have fallen off of warships

And sank to the bottom of the Atlantic Ocean in the past twenty years

And the entire world as well as a billion or so fish

Are waiting for them to explode.

Korea's a mess and South Africa's repressed and England's unemployed.

Beirut's a big pile of rubble because a few separate factions

Read different authors.

And in the Southeast section of Washington, D.C.,

An eighteen year-old in a van

Ripped apart a mother and child with an Uzi

Because his brain was bleeding with crack.

Eggplant Rufus

But a friend called me on that day when I was done

Reading the newspaper

And enlightened me with a truly positive observation

On this twisted rock in space.

"You know," he said,

"Black girls look great in tight blue dresses."

Indeed, as old Louie Armstrong would say,

What a wonderful world.

Yard Sale Saturday

Sometimes when the sun is shining and the air is fresh,

American families will tote their less useful belongings

Out to their front yards and attempt to diminish their clutter

By selling these items to their neighbors at prices only a fool would refuse.

Who could turn down a fully functional stationary bike

With only a few minor defects for the paltry sum of two dollars?

It's America in all of its capitalist glory and we call it a yard sale.

Today is one such Saturday and I am stumbling

Through a stranger's yard learning a lot about them as I poke

Through tidbits of their history which they now are quite comfortable

With having someone else own.

Little red, yellow, and green stickers are pasted announcing the

Rock bottom prices for which I can take home old board games,

Coffee tables, paperback novels, piles of winter scarves and mittens,

And many other once prized possessions.

As I wander through the assortment, I am overtaken by a kind of funky,

Yard sale lateral gravity that beckons me to a pile of men's underpants

That sits proudly on a bent-legged card table.

What on Earth, I wonder to myself, possesses a family to put

Generations of briefs and boxers up for public scrutiny?

I begin fumbling through the collection –

There are blue boxers with the words "eat me" stenciled over the crotch,

A set of orange Halloween briefs with a curious hole in the

Nose of the Jack O' Lantern,

Eggplant Rufus

And – most disturbing and hidden near the bottom of the heap –
A ripped pair of Fruit-of-the-Looms garnished
With nearly a twelve-inch poop stain from one end to the other.
I drop them immediately as if a tarantula has crawled out from them
And move away from the scene.
I look back to see the small sign which reads, "Five dollars takes all"
Next to the underwear collection.
My yard sale stamina is exhausted and I make my way back to the car.
I look back at the scene once again just in time
To see an older couple scoop up the entire stack of underwear
And present it to the homeowner with a crisp new
Five-dollar bill for payment.
The bundle of underpants is placed in an old grocery store bag
And the couple walks away quite contented with their purchase.
I am amazed to bear witness, I think, to such a precise little metaphor
Of life on Earth this yard sale has yielded on this fine spring Saturday.
One can see that element of the unknown that makes both yard sales
And life itself an unpredictable endeavor.
How often have we all felt that glorious moment of elation
When we have learned that five dollars can buy you a near mountain
Of underwear,
Only to have that joy tarnished when you became aware
Some time later that the same five-dollar bill additionally acquired
Someone else's foot-long poop stain?

Kamikaze Argument

They had an argument on the telephone today

And now he is angry

Because he knows she is right,

Not perhaps about this singular issue

But about every issue and all issues

That lead to subsequent issues

That sets in motion every discussion

And leads inevitably to arguments

Such as the one just concluded

On the telephone.

He is angrier still because he knows this,

Because he knows that he is wrong,

That his position was weak before the argument began,

And yet, he continued to hold his ground

Stupidly,

Like walking on the beach at Normandy

And standing still in the surf

While the Germans tear up the sand with machine guns

Around his feet

Or charging across the field

With George Pickett at Gettysburg

And holding a Neon flag that says "Shoot me."

He entered into the argument

With no expectations of victory or survival -

Eggplant Rufus

A kamikaze pilot with a telephone,

Crashing his plane into her battleship

Every day, day after day,

When the war is already lost.

Hairbrush Microphone

No one knew there was a big concert that night

In my small little suburban town.

But from ten pm until approximately midnight,

The glam band Queen appeared in my bedroom

Playing every hit from "Bohemian Rhapsody" to "Fat Bottomed Girls."

I had headphones and a hairbrush for a microphone,

And for two hours I was Freddie Mercury,

Dancing across the stage and waving my arms in performance bravado

And rubbing back to back with Brian May as he wailed out

The guitar solo on "Killer Queen."

The concert was interrupted only briefly when my sister walked in

And pointed at me laughing,

But I couldn't hear what she said

As my ears were swelling with a Roger Taylor drum solo.

Freddie Mercury was my hero,

And so was Rock Hudson,

The hip detective from the Rockford Files who had also

Single-handedly taken out the scheming, untrustable Russians

In "Ice Station Zebra."

I knew this was a fact because I had seen it for myself with my Dad

At a United Artist theatre in the early 1970's and after the movie

My father took me to K-mart and bought me a plastic model

Of the submarine that Rock had used to penetrate the polar ice cap.

I constructed that submarine and re-created that scene

Eggplant Rufus

Through ice cubes in the bath tub until I inevitably set the submarine

On fire one rainy summer day.

Freddie and Rock,

Now these were men of substance – these were heroes.

Years later I learned they were both gay as the day is long

And that Rock himself was even hooking up with Gomer Pyle, USMC.

I was a grown man when I heard the news

And it didn't change my opinion about these childhood heroes in any way.

I knew for a fact that it wouldn't have mattered

To me years before

As a fourth grader on a Saturday night in my bedroom

Where I could be found

A little high on the airplane glue used to construct an

Authentic replica of Rock's nuclear-powered submarine,

And dripping with sweat from a first-class impersonation

Of Freddie Mercury.

How they lived their lives didn't mean squat at all,

Rock and Freddie were much more than that to me:

They were the fuel for my ten year-old imagination as

I fought the Russians and rocked packed arenas,

With a tube of model cement

And a hairbrush microphone.

Deja Moo

The bulky Hereford strolled lazily through her world,

A flat, rock-strewn stretch of farmland

At the foot of a chain of mountains

That ran from one end of the continent to the other.

She stopped at a charcoal boulder

Left there one million years before by a meandering glacier.

Skirting the bottom of the rock

Were tall and meaty blades of fine new grass

Poking their pointed heads towards

The blue late afternoon sky.

The cow bent and slowly,

Thoughtfully,

Tugged at several blades of grass

And began to chew.

A single black fly hovered around the Hereford's left ear,

Landing first on the bony outgrowth which held the spotted flap

And then, finally,

Settled on the tip of the cow's nose.

She crossed her eyes to have a look at the fly

Who was busily grooming with hectic motions

Of forearm to face.

The cow's eyes narrowed and her brain focused

On a means of encouraging this unwanted guest

To perform the ritualistic maintenance cleaning

Eggplant Rufus

Elsewhere.

The Hereford realized that there was indeed no solution at all,

That she would have to be content to have this little guest

On her nose until it chose to fly off

To another destination.

At that moment,

The cow shuddered and felt a deep chill run through her spine,

And dropped a wad of partially-chewed grass

From her mouth to the ground.

She remembered a similar, almost too similar,

Dilemma

The day before, or the week before,

Or had it all been a dream?

At that instant this Hereford knew that somewhere,

Some time,

This had all happened before.

Friend in Space

I wish I could meet an astronaut

Before he or she took off for a mission.

I would like to talk to one at a dinner party,

And find some common ground -

Maybe a sports team we both like,

Or an old disco song we both find intolerable.

Then, when they shot him into space,

I could walk outside the house one night and

Look into the sky and think,

Hey, there's that guy who doesn't like "I Will Survive"

By Gloria Gaynor.

I would actually know someone hurtling around the Earth

Above my head and

During the day while I was at work,

I could think that -

Wow -

Far above the roof of this old building

Up past the stars and where the day turns into black,

There's old Henry there.

And I know he can't stand the Dallas Cowboys,

Just like me.

It would be great if one of my friends were an astronaut,

But I don't have any friends that are even close.

Many are just 9-to-5 working stiffs like me,

Or lawyers, ten-cent entrepreneurs, whatever.

None of them are astronauts.

I suppose I could have been an astronaut myself,

That would take the whole problem away.

But I never was that interested in science and anyway,

The grass is always greener -

I know as soon as I was an astronaut

I would be wishing I had a friend

Who worked in a cubicle.

Bowling Night

I was a young lobbyist spending nights at fundraisers and then

Heading to a local political watering hole for nightcaps with legislators

And other professionals involved in the business of government.

It was at this tavern on Wednesday nights

Where a white-haired old man would pass around Polaroid photos

Of neatly shaved anonymous vaginas,

Pubic surgery he had performed himself only hours before.

You see it was this gentleman's "bowling night" as he told his wife,

And instead of heading to an alley and rolling a sixteen pound ball,

This sixty-something would call one of half a dozen

Regularly utilized prostitutes and meet them at a local motel.

He would bring with him two hundred dollars, a shaving kit,

And a Polaroid camera.

And for his one-hour of prepaid service, he would set about to eliminate

Every sprouting hair from his partner's genitalia.

He would then snap photos and bring them to the bar

To show anyone even mildly interested.

As a political newbie, I asked obvious questions to this curious regular,

"How long have you been doing this?"

He told me quite proudly, "Twenty years."

"And your wife believes you're actually bowling every Wednesday?"

He smirked and responded, "Well to help legitimize the alibi,

Every three months or so I buy myself a trophy."

I asked him to photograph his trophy shelf, and sure enough,

Eggplant Rufus

A week later he showed me three shelves stuffed with trophies of all sizes,

Each, in my eyes, representing countless shaven vaginas.

I stopped being a lobbyist a few years later,

About the time this gentleman and his wife were invited

To their seven-year old grandson's birthday bowling party.

His wife, the hopeful participatory grandparent,

Volunteered her husband to keep score for everyone,

After all, he had bowled in a league for twenty-five years.

It became apparent to his wife and everyone at the party

That this "league" bowler certainly knew nothing about bowling –

His scorekeeping was of his own creation –

Five hundred points for a strike

And an inconsistent, random number of points for a spare.

The final scores were in the thousands for ten bowled frames

And many of the parents at the party looked oddly at the results

Of his efforts.

When the party ended,

His wife went home and spent an hour rifling the roll-top desk in his office

Above the garage and found three thousand photographs

Of hairless vaginas.

It was then that she determined it was time to pack her bags and

Spend the remaining twenty years of her life looking for a man

Who was honest, caring,

And didn't bowl.

Broccoli Feedback

She is thirty-four

And in love with a stockbroker from Long Island

She has known for three weeks.

She is enraptured.

They sit in a Greenwich Village bistro

Talking about art.

He opens up - she loves this about him -

And admits he never really understood Picasso.

She smiles

And belches softly under her breath.

Suddenly,

The two small pieces of raw broccoli

She consumed at lunch

With a light sour cream and dill weed dip

Re-emerge with a powerful vengeance

In the form of a horrifying cloud of

Undigested green vegetable stench that hovers between them.

He stands up and exits the restaurant never to return and

Leaving her to regret

The painful decision she made

Earlier in the day when she was attracted to the sizeable

Stalks resting enticingly like crispy, green brains

Atop her lunchtime tossed salad.

"I'll never eat broccoli again," she laments,

Eggplant Rufus

As a soft, lonely rain

Taps a melancholy refrain

On the bistro window.

Hateful Chapin

In 1974, I was riding in my mother's car to school

And remember hearing the song "Cat's in the Cradle."

No, it wasn't as cool to me as "Crocodile Rock" or "Space Oddity"

But it had a nice chorus that I had memorized

And would sing along annoyingly to the AM radio.

I was too young to pick up the vibe about a father

Not spending enough time with his son in the song,

I just hummed along with the lyrics,

"We'll get together then, son,

I know we'll have a good time then."

In 1981 while on my way to a summertime high school party,

I learned that Harry Chapin had been driving on the

Long Island Expressway and veered his 1975 Volkswagen Rabbit

In front of tractor trailer which caused his car's gas tank to rupture

And burst into flames.

For a month the radio stations played "Cat's in a Cradle"

Repeatedly to memorialize Harry,

And every day several times you heard the words,

"When ya coming home Dad, I don't know when,

We'll get together then, son."

Now I'm standing in a Denver airport in a security line

Twenty-five years after Harry Chapin drove that Rabbit

Into Heaven on the Long Island Expressway,

And that song is blasting through the airport loudspeakers.

Eggplant Rufus

I am flying from Denver to Chicago today as part of a week-long

Business trip that will end with two short days at home

Before getting in my car and driving to Louisville, Kentucky

For a five-day convention.

I can hear the song echoing through the airport right now

And all I can think is

"Fuck you, Harry Chapin,"

As I envision my boys sitting at home

And I am wishing I was there to throw baseballs and footballs

With them in our back yard.

Fuck you, hateful Chapin,

For giving me this song as I stand a thousand miles away from my own kids

And knowing that I will see them for forty-eight hours

In a couple of days

Before I have to leave them for another week.

And while I am at it,

Fuck you Denver airport for playing this song –

Good lord don't you know so many of the people standing in torturous

Security lines have themselves just muttered

Long distance promises to their own children,

Promises like, "We'll get together then, son."

I am on the cell phone with my own family when the song finally ends,

And all I can think about as I thumb the button to end the call is,

"I know we'll have a good time then..."

Mildred's Magic Carpet

My neighbor when I was young

Was a seventy-something woman named Mildred,

And every day she would wave to me when I walked home

From school.

She was always sitting on a folding chair on her porch,

And her husband Al would be puttering around in the garage

With some tool or the other making noises that sounded like progress.

I never knew much about either one of them

Except every year at Christmas we had to go over to their house

And they would give my sister and I a pair of pajamas.

I never liked pajamas much,

But it was hard to say that on Christmas eve when you never knew

For certain whether any last indiscretion could cost you presents

The next morning.

The most endearing quality about Mildred was her inability

To close her legs when seated,

As if it were her life's work to expose second-grade boys

To her genitals on a daily basis.

Her perch three steps up on her front porch was exactly eye-level

For any kid walking past on the sidewalk,

So we were always visually-aligned

With what we later nicknamed "Mildred's Magic Carpet."

No matter what brand of underpants Mildred pulled on in the morning,

There was never enough cloth to provide adequate coverage

Eggplant Rufus

Or concealment of what could best be described

As a beehive hairdo between her legs.

We boys speculated that it was the sheer volume of hair

That forced her legs to be permanently agape.

We learned to look up and wave very quickly when passing her chair,

And to not look at the hive for fear of turning to stone.

Her vagina was our adolescent Medusa all foreboding and mysterious,

A great Odyssean challenge to overcome on a daily basis.

New kids to the neighborhood were never warned,

And were in fact encouraged to look closely

As they might see something

Magical.

When they subsequently made eye contact,

Their shock became our hilarity.

But there was something refreshing and safe about that genital jungle,

It might have been horrific,

But it was home.

Sometimes when I had been away on a vacation,

It never seemed as if I was really "home" until I had

Slept in my own bed,

Thrown a tennis ball against the brick wall beside my house

And got a big fat eye full of

Mildred's magic carpet.

Macaroni Snow

Looking outside and there is some macaroni snow

On the ground.

On Sunday,

Just four days ago,

The weather predictors told us all on the east coast

Of the United States

That we were to get pelted with a blizzard that could easily

Be the precursor to the next ice age.

Over the course of Monday and Tuesday,

It snowed a total of two inches.

Now everyone is angry at the weather prognosticators

For pushing a panic button that didn't need to be pushed.

Schools closed, businesses shut down, citizens rushed

Grocery stores for emergency supplies,

Then waited in their houses

While looking out their windows and seeing nothing happen.

Now it is Wednesday,

And there is still some snow on the ground.

It isn't the two or three feet that was predicted,

It is the tenacious remnants of a two-inch dusting.

Meanwhile all across town,

Folks are sitting in their homes and

Staring at dozens of rolls of emergency toilet paper

And more milk than they ever could hope to consume.

Eggplant Rufus

I am looking at the little gathering of snow right now,

And thinking that it has no idea what trouble it caused,

Like the dinner guest who thinks he's doing you a favor

By getting a sitter for his kids

After you have already prepared a separate casserole

Of macaroni and cheese just for the little tykes.

Oh, it's still just fine to see your old friend,

But since you boiled the macaroni and made the casserole,

He might have just as well

Brought the damn kids.

Sweet Perspective

Life is a series of random, inexplicable and unexpected events.

For instance:

An out-of-towner was run over at a Friendly's restaurant

By a kid and his girlfriend in his Dad's Ford Taurus.

He never expected it.

A tragic juxtaposition – killed in a place called "Friendly's."

He never even ate and died hungry.

Similarly,

A Japanese man was bent over in his garden delicately

Tending to his shrubbery

At eight in the morning one August day in 1945.

He gently tugged at a weed that was threatening the roots

Of a nearby rose bush,

When he felt a flash of unearthly heat

And became a vaporized shadow on the side of a concrete

Wall of his home.

He never expected it.

He must have thought he had pulled

A weed from hell.

And consider this:

An accountant worked a second job dressing as a clown

For children's parties on weekends.

Zippy the clown, he called himself.

He worked a nine-year old's birthday party one Saturday afternoon

And some villainous kid set the cuffs of his multi-colored pants

On fire with a lighter.

He never expected it.

Zippy met Zippo,

And the rest of his outfit went up like flash paper.

They removed his body with a vacuum cleaner.

So then, here I am,

At an inner city stop light which has finally turned green,

And the woman in front of me in the mini-van is turned around

And yelling at her children in the back seat.

She doesn't see the light has changed.

She yells at the children all the way through

The green light, the shorter yellow light,

And well into the ensuing red light.

I want to open the door of my car, walk over to hers

And drag her out on to the street for her transgression.

Then, for some reason,

I think about that hungry man in the Friendly's parking lot,

And that Hiroshima gardener,

And that dead clown,

And decide instead to forgive that pre-occupied woman

And wait for the next green light.

Ah, perspective,

Sweet perspective.

Clouds

Two young lovers are lying on their backs

In a beautiful green field

Gazing

Into a herd of motionless clouds.

"That cloud," says the man,

"Looks like the gates of Heaven opening up

In all of their splendor

With the warming hands of the Lord

Beckoning

The two of us into his Eternal Domain

As an everlasting example of what true love

Is

And could be

And should be

Forever."

He kisses his lover on the cheek,

As she scratches at her chin and looks

To the sky above

And whispers softly,

"I don't know,

That cloud looks

Like a dog

Taking a shit to me."

She points straight into the cumulus mass,

Eggplant Rufus

"See, honey, there is his tail
And there is the turd."
The man looks again with a squint
And says,
"Yes it does, yes it does."
They would later be married,
And remain happily so
For the rest of their lives.

Hair Salon Soliloquy

She cuts my hair for half an hour and chews gum

With relentless intensity and asks a lot of questions

About my life and career and previous barbers and hair stylists

And the truly creative failures they have performed on my curly locks

To leave my head in the sad state

In which it now exists.

Those previous barbers and hairstylists worked their unfortunate magic

In malls and barbershops and hotels

Where they whacked with clippers and buzzed with razors

And raked with combs and blew with dryers

And moussed with mousse

Only to leave me here now with my new savior, my new shining light,

Who assures me that my random odyssey of hair maintenance

Would end now once I see the wonders that she will perform.

Then she speaks about the weather outside and her plans for the evening

And further plans for the next day and about a vacation she will be taking

At the end of the month and I lose any hope of a peaceful

Hair experience and realize that she will talk

Ceaselessly until I leave her chair.

She speaks of growing up and high school and her progression

Through hair styling school

After taking a brief and unsuccessful crack at modeling in her late teens.

I am certain at one point during her monologue

The gum falls out of her mouth and into my hair

But she deftly clips it away without allowing me enough time to say,

"Hey, is there gum in my hair?"

She continues speaking and speaking and speaking

And even when the blow dryer

Hums loudly she continues talking and I am fairly sure

She is speculating aloud about whether or not she should take up the cello

Or if instead a more preferable musical instrument for her would be

The piano.

Now she holds the mirror behind my head to show me how the back of the

Style looks, and I think, "I can't see the back of my head anyway."

She asks me what I think of her work,

And the only thing I can think to say is, "Stupendous."

She is gleeful and we head to the counter where I pay

And give her a five-dollar tip while she hands me her business card and

Implores me to call her in advance to set up my next appointment.

I walk out the door of the salon and toss the card into a trashcan

In an effort to avoid a future felony on my part,

Because I know for a fact that if I subjected myself to her discussions again

I would bury a pair of shears into her neck at some point during the haircut.

I look back and she is smiling and waving out of the front window and

I wave meekly back

And think to myself,

"Oh darling, I have just saved your fucking life."

Old Man at McDonald's

There's an old man at McDonald's

Sitting alone in the first booth

By the entrance.

He is looking out the window

At the mounting traffic in the parking lot.

It is six o'clock and the dinner crowd

Is racing toward the door.

There are children and parents

And older couples groping with coupons clipped

From the Sunday paper

And mini-vans in the drive-thru filled with

Little league baseball teams.

The old man is folding the yellow wrapper

Of a cheeseburger

He has already eaten –

Folding the wrapper neatly into a tiny square

And staring through time

To a day when he hated fast food restaurants

And would nearly run home from work

To smell his wife's cooking.

He thinks back to a moment

Fifty years earlier when he and his new bride

Dined at a local phenomenon called "McDonald's"

For the first time

And he said to her, "This kind of restaurant will never succeed."

He hears her reply,

"Whatever you say, honey,"

Just as she said it that day,

And he feels the warmth of her hand squeezing his

As they pull out of the parking lot

And on to the new interstate highway.

In the restaurant today,

An adolescent sitting at a nearby table

Points across the room at the old man

And says to his sister,

"He must be a crazy old coot,"

She nods in agreement

While taking a bite of her hamburger.

And why shouldn't she agree with her brother,

For there the old man sits

Staring into space

And smiling.

Buffet Virtuosos

It is a lazy Saturday lunch and I stop at an establishment
Famous for its buffet.
It is one of the many such restaurants that keep their buffet out all day -
Breakfast, lunch and dinner.
It is the twenty-first century, mind you, and we have all been warned
Repeatedly
About the problems associated with a high-fat diet.
Those warnings echo unheard throughout the brightly lit corridors
Of this human grazing maze -
Stations of every fat-laden concoction known to man are loaded
Into stainless steel pans and offered steaming to the salivating masses.
The food, by and large, is awful - but the customers seem not to notice –
As they amble up to the offerings like an insect to an alluring scent.
A herd of four three-hundred-plus pounders saunters purposefully
Up to the feeding area and acquire empty plates.
Using the dish very much like an artist's canvas, they create a gathering of
Culinary garbage that fills the vessel nearly to the brim,
Then trudge back to their booth,
Proudly carting back their edible masterpieces.
The subsequent consumption is accomplished with Olympian rapidity,
Yet the Salisbury steaks, the fried chicken, the miniature corn dogs,
Nearly all taste the same.
It is not so much epicurean satisfaction that is measured here,
Rather the quantity and speed with which the empty,

Eggplant Rufus

Gravy-painted plates accumulate.

The depleted plates will be removed by a sweating, underpaid

High School student working to buy a new MP-3 player

To download pirate mpegs from the worldwide web.

A curious entry into this self-contained universe,

He's a ghastly thin teenager with a bolt through his lip,

But he knows enough to individually ask each

Of these clearly obese forty-somethings

If they were finished before gently removing their plates from the table.

I make my own voyage to the food line,

And return lamenting the behavior of the group.

I had waited patiently to grab a hold of the spoon that

Would shovel some questionable meat loaf on my plate,

When a buffet virtuoso jumped in front of me

And procured the last steaming slab.

No words were spoken in the exchange, and at once I realized

I need to allow these veterans their free reign.

This very world within these walls which they call their own

More than likely hastens their exit from the world outside these walls.

So for here and now,

This is their domain, their own symphony of gluttony,

And I am only a confused and ill-prepared

Guest.

Hammertoe

As if she didn't have enough problems already,

Eleanor thought while rolling out of bed on a Tuesday morning.

It was raining, cold and the middle of November -

Her least favorite month -

And on top of it all,

She had this damned

Hammertoe.

It is an affliction too often ignored in today's society -

But can any of us afford to continue to discount

This painful malformation of the second, third or fourth toes

Caused by wearing too-tight pumps and fancy heels?

There appears to be no cure for the dreaded hammertoe

And no urgent search to find one.

There are no celebrity spokesmen, no holiday stamps, no telethons.

Have we ever really acknowledged the sacrifices of so many

Who bear the unspeakable pain of torturous footwear

So that we may all benefit from the accentuation these shoes provide

To calves, thighs and buttocks,

Or the additional inch or two or three of height?

Clearly, those of us who are enriched from the results

Should take the time to say a heartfelt

"Thank you."

Perhaps we should open our wallets for a research effort,

Or divert funding from less necessary causes

To develop a user-friendly stiletto.

But these advances are well in the future –

For today,

There is only painful and lonely suffering,

As on this particular rainy November morning

When another unhappy victim

Must limp gingerly to the closet

And sadly choose her flats.

Happier Days

When he returned to the classroom after acquiring his bathroom pass,

Everyone could see that the new kid had urinated in his pants.

A dark stain stretched below his beltline and down below his knees.

It was wonderful.

Later, in the same class,

He would fall off his chair and the teacher would walk towards him

To assess the situation,

And as she pulled him gently back up to his seat,

He would projectile vomit across three rows of students.

It was spectacular.

For all of his issues that day,

The boy was sent to the nurse's office

And then finally

Home.

It was all so wonderful then,

Those happier days.

When you barfed in class,

A janitor just threw sawdust on it and the school sent you home.

And when you pissed your pants,

Your mother brought you another pair.

And we who watched the urinating and vomiting still had our laughs

And I bet the teachers huddled in their smoking lounges

And had a giggle too.

I can still fondly recall that feeling of complete exhilaration

Eggplant Rufus

When a classmate suddenly vomited –

It was as if the world had stopped spinning,

As if the orderly nature of the classroom had been turned upside down.

Time stood still.

Sometimes, to compound the entertainment,

Other students would vomit in response.

Good Lord where did that joy go?

Now that we are older,

Seeing someone vomit isn't funny anymore.

Instead of "wahoo!",

You are more likely to hear "Dear God!"

What the hell happened?

Where did we lose that sense of delight in the simple things?

I wonder where you are now,

All the pukers and urinators who made our school days

Such little adventures.

I need you now in business meetings

Or presentations to groups of strangers

Or even in too-long holiday gatherings with relatives.

The invitation is always open,

My little grade-school entertainers –

Bring your weak bladders and upset stomachs

And I'll bring the sawdust.

Mouse Suicide Note

Goodbye cruel masonry,

Sayonara studs.

This is all she wrote for this mouse.

I'm sick of the hours

And I have had it

With the fucking cat.

Squeak.

Pepperoni Optimism

She walks from the curb to the landing

Of the pizzeria

And sees a young vagrant with shifty eyes.

"I love you," he tells her,

And she dashes back to her car horrified

And drives away at top speed vowing never

To eat at that pizza place again.

The young vagrant meant every word he said:

He has been watching her from an alley

Every day

For the last eleven months.

She comes at lunchtime,

And he sees her graceful movements as she

Gently pulls herself from her car and walks into

The restaurant,

Then re-emerges ten minutes later with

A small box within which he imagined was

A small pepperoni pizza or stromboli.

He had thought about what he would say

The moment he met her,

How he would sum up his longing and feelings

For her.

He gathered his strength and his courage

Day after day,

Eggplant Rufus

Until this fateful day when he finally said,

"This is it"

And left his alley home to say those words

"I love you"

While bathing in the deep scent of her perfume

Mixed with the distinctive odor of pepperoni.

There was that moment,

He thought, that millisecond before she ran frightened

To her car when their eyes met

And he knew that the next time he said

"I love you"

She would say the same back to him.

Tomorrow, he thinks to himself,

Is going to be that day.

Halfway across town now,

The woman has pulled in front of a Chinese takeout joint

And remembers how much she has always loved

Won ton soup.

Midnight in La Jolla

Damn it the drinks are expensive in this little

Jewel town by the Pacific.

It appears to be the playground of the rich

But in my corner of the bar

There is a Limp Bizkit song playing on the jukebox

And a middle-aged man mumbling to an obvious prostitute.

He says, "I like to suck tits" as if it were a declaration of love.

She puts her chewing gum in a bar napkin

And gives him a kiss as he mumbles,

"I'm so fat, so awfully fat...why are you even talking to me?"

She is at work using all of her skills

And whispers "you're not fat" to him.

He clearly has not recognized that unlike traditional

Romantic relationships,

The one he is currently initiating could be instantly advanced

To the stage of sexual intimacy

With an infusion of cash.

I would like to see how this little story ends

But I am out of money

And walk outside to where the trees are strewn

With sparkling white lights.

There is a twenty-something man puking beside a vending machine

That sells a newspaper describing the San Diego nightlife.

A few feet from where his vomit hits the pavement

Eggplant Rufus

Is an exclusive gallery selling indistinguishable crystalline structures

For $7500.

I look in the window and I think, "That looks like an elephant"

While the young man continues puking behind me.

I look back across the street at the bar

To see the fat man who likes to suck tits and the prostitute

Who doesn't think he's fat

Leaving arm in arm.

It's midnight in La Jolla, California, and with the acrid scent of upchuck

Mixing with the Pacific Ocean breeze,

I am thinking of those who travel here to feel for a moment

Like they belong in this tiny village of affluence.

For me, my memories will include only vomit and crystal sculptures

I could neither afford nor recognize.

But for one man across the street and his professional accomplice,

His La Jolla memories will consist of those nipples

He so openly craves,

And a newfound belief that despite what his reflection might disclose

In any serviceable mirror,

He may not be so damned fat after all.

Potato Salad

My best friend's girl was a real mean one,

A real piece of work.

When he came home late in the evening

She always yelled at him.

Really!

On weekends, she inevitably expected some kind of getaway,

You know – like a quiet picnic by the lake.

"A picnic," he complained,

"Always a damned picnic!"

I kid you not,

She was a complete freaking bitch, this one.

"My old lady has got to go,"

He said to me as we cowered over our mugs last Tuesday night

At the tavern.

Just like that, you see –

That's all he told me, honestly.

When my friend went home that evening,

He woke his girlfriend out of a sound sleep

Tied her arms and legs securely,

Stuffed a rolled up tube sock in her mouth,

Taped it shut,

Threw her in the trunk of his Thunderbird,

Drove three days to Flagstaff, Arizona,

And then left her in a field next to a lake in the middle of a

Eggplant Rufus

Seldom-used state park.

He then turned the Thunderbird around and drove home.

At this point,

She was hungry, tired and dirty,

Fifteen hundred miles away from home

And considerably lost.

But she wasn't angry,

Just a little sad

To be left alone in such a beautiful place

On a peaceful summer day

Overlooking a small lake,

And to be there

Without a bottle of white wine,

A red-checkered tablecloth

And potato salad.

Dead Crap Trilogy

Stains

I saw you sitting there with some ugly Parisian prostitute

Sipping a warm Kronenborg and flashing that gold molar.

You didn't know me,

But two hours earlier I saw you beat three

Dobermans to death with a lead pipe

In Pigalle

Four blocks from my hotel.

So now it's past midnight in Paris

And your hand is on her thigh

And I bet you don't know there is Doberman blood on your shirt.

There is.

Thank God it's Paris

And you can pay for it.

First Dead Robin of Springtime

This year I saw it in the second week of May

Mulched to oblivion in the parking lot of a mall.

It was the first dead robin of springtime and I knew at that moment

That my wool suits had to go into storage.

Once I saw it on the third day of April,

Some yuppie was pulling it out of the grill of his BMW at a car wash.

"Save that," I said, "it's the first dead robin of springtime."

He looked at me unamused.

"What are you, some kind of retard?" he said.

Maybe so, I thought, but I'm comfortable.

In 1984, I waited so long to see one that I desperately

Investigated crow and dove corpses for even a hint of a red breast.

Finally, in July,

A mail truck clipped one in front of my house

And with a satisfied smile

I removed my cashmere topcoat.

Wheat Thins, Mouse Traps and Beans

Cans of beans,

Three, in fact, cans of beans

On the shelf below

The shelf

Upon which rests

The cocked and deadly trap

For the unscrupulous mouse

That the evening before

Defiantly dined on my box

Of Wheat Thins.

Sea Monkeys and Corned Beef Hash

Sea monkeys are tiny pellets of supposedly dehydrated aquatic animals

Which, according to the box they came in, would resemble when fully grown

Tiny seahorses with long eyelashes, ape faces and human arms.

This was too much temptation for any kid and I would have my parents buy

Them for me every year on our annual road trip to Florida.

The trip would always end in Miami where,

At a restaurant shaped like a big hat,

You could eat blueberry muffins and patties of corned beef hash

That were the best things in the world.

Another benefit of this restaurant was that every kid that walked

Through the door would receive an Archie comic book as a gift -

Primarily to keep the kids quiet while the parents ate breakfast.

At night we would play shuffleboard at our motel on the beach

And I would hate to lose,

But we always had ice cream afterwards at a shop downtown.

The roadside stands sold fresh orange juice and coconut milk

And for two weeks every year I didn't have to worry about

Math or spelling or social studies, my only concern was winning the nightly

Shuffleboard game, the thickness of the milk shakes in the coffee shop,

And – most importantly – whether the sea monkeys would come to life

Or just float around like so much fish food for the entire vacation.

One year our week in Florida coincided

With my ninth birthday and on my special day,

With the sea monkeys sitting in a water-filled ice bucket

Eggplant Rufus

On the television set in our room,

We dressed ourselves in our best Floridian clothes and headed

For the big hat restaurant for breakfast.

When we had taken our seat, the waitress handed each one of us a menu,

But I noticed she had forgotten my Archie comic book.

"We only give them out to the little, little boys," she explained.

My God, I thought, I am nine

And I am an old man.

For some reason, right after that exchange with the waitress,

The corned beef hash didn't taste that great at all

And when we returned to the room

I knew for the first time that those sea monkeys would never come to life.

Today, you can get killed in Miami in the same places

Where we played shuffleboard and ate corned beef hash.

It's all drugs and gangs now and those guys don't have time

To wait for sea monkeys to evolve.

My children will never see the Miami Beach I remember.

A shame for them, I suppose,

But for me,

Well I will always happily recall being eight years old in Miami –

And the feeling of wonderful anticipation

And nerve-wracking mystery

That surrounded my annual experiment with sea monkeys

And the glorious taste

Of corned beef hash.

Throw a Bone

The battle of the sexes will rage forever

As long as there are men and there are women.

At least that's what I am thinking tonight -

Sitting alone at a bar in a Virginia nightclub watching a couple dance

And scrawling these words on a cocktail napkin.

The dancing couple are not married,

They probably met somewhere earlier and ended up here.

He's older than she is -

In his mid-forties, a little overweight and middle management for life.

She is pushing thirty, a little Latin in the face and

Wearing tight designer jeans - probably a paralegal.

They are the only couple on the dance floor and she is very drunk.

He is stupid, of course –

He bought the shots of tequila that made her this way.

I watched her down two consecutive infusions of the Mexican gasoline

And her eyes rolled back in her head each time.

With each shot of alcohol, he lost a little more control over her -

The big fish was taking more line and swimming further from the boat.

So now they are dancing.

Well he is dancing at least - a little white man's shuffle from side to side.

Meanwhile, she is all

Exaggerated movements and flapping arms and grandiose twists,

An audition for every man in the club.

She is not so much dancing as she is performing.

Eggplant Rufus

"Look at my body," she says with her gestures,

"Look at my ass, isn't this what you want?"

I'm reaching for a fresh napkin when she falls for the first time

And her partner dutifully picks her up so she can continue the display.

There will be two more falls before the song is over.

The couple leaves hastily, the man pays the check and

Puts his arm around her shoulder and guides her out the front door.

I watch their car back out of the parking lot and I think to myself

Wow, men just act, think and behave like gorillas

And women behave, think and perform like actresses.

The gorillas act and react and grab their testicles and jump up and down

And the actresses put on artificial performances to attract

These brainless primates.

I was somehow hoping we would all be further evolved by now,

And I think of the scene in "2001: A Space Odyssey"

When the apes took that next step in evolution by learning that a bone

Is a perfectly useful device for bludgeoning one's enemies.

What will be our bone, I wonder

As I sit here in this smelly Virginia nightclub?

If that is all it takes,

Then for the love of God,

Someone throw us one

Fucking bone.

Cicada Vacation

It is a summertime afternoon in Washington, D.C.,

And the cicadas are back in full force.

I am sitting at a red light and there are millions of them flying around

And bouncing off cars or seemingly dropping dead in mid-air

And falling on to sidewalks, streets and cars.

I switch on my wipers to chase off a dozen cicadas resting or dying

On my windshield and blocking my vision.

It is hot, and my air conditioning now doesn't work,

So I roll down the window for some breeze and I'm immediately

Assaulted by a renegade squadron of cicadas,

Now bouncing around my car in the back seat.

A few minutes later they are seemingly all gone,

And I continue driving down the George Washington Parkway

Heading towards Alexandria.

There are two kinds of cicadas in the United States –

One variety lives underground for thirteen years,

The other for seventeen.

As if by some unknown signal, each species of cicada emerges above the

Ground at once, living for thirty or forty days,

Mating, laying eggs and then dying a week or so later.

So there it is for you, underground for thirteen or seventeen years,

Waiting for that month of freedom.

And here I am now driving through Alexandria and another patch of cicadas,

When I see a woman in a Chanel dress walking purposefully

Eggplant Rufus

Down the street,

A sizeable cicada lodged on her left buttock and bouncing up and down

As if it were his private insect amusement park.

What the hell, I think, you've waited seventeen years – enjoy the ride.

The next day I begin my drive home from Washington,

An easy ninety-minute cruise to my chunk of Pennsylvania suburbia.

A few miles from my house, I hear a melodious chirping from the back seat -

And there sits a cicada left over from the previous day's invasion.

He has now crossed state lines.

I knew that he had sacrificed much to be above ground,

And wouldn't have long to enjoy the view.

The back seat of my car just wouldn't do.

So instead of going directly home, I drove that cicada to an island in the

Middle of a river and opened the back door.

He looked at me as he sat in the back seat and I swear

He winked.

Then he jumped out and walked across the parking lot to the water's edge.

I drove away happy with how it had all turned out –

That cicada had waited underground seventeen years for this.

Maybe he's not with his pack, maybe he won't find another cicada,

So be it.

Yes, maybe I couldn't get that cicada laid during his forty-day visit to Earth,

But at least I got him

To the damned beach.

Manhattan Krishna

It is midday in Manhattan

And the Times Square sun is burning the glistening baldness

On the top of your head.

The tail of hair behind your neck is impeccably tied

And the white robe adorning your skeleton frame is bleached blinding.

Only the red high-top sneakers indicate any sense of turmoil

On this placid scene of devotion as your right hand

Methodically

Taps

A hand-made bongo.

You pick your way through the afternoon New York throng,

Past a subway entrance

Where a woman of eighty sits on a Marshall amplifier

And plays an electric guitar singing

"I want to live with a cinnamon girl."

Past the eight black children bashing trash can lids and boxes

In rhythm

While a group of secretaries on break applaud and giggle.

Past the cabbie who yells

"Fuck you zipperhead!" to a Chinese man on a bicycle.

And past the Indian selling incense for three and a quarter

That will

"Intensify your meditation" and "relax your weary soul, brother."

I catch up to you at a "don't walk" sign by a Cuban vendor

Eggplant Rufus

Peddling fruit in a plastic cup

And I notice that you must be my age.

I envision you as a young boy watching

"Deputy Dawg" and "The Flintstones"

And can see you laughing when Fred and Barney

Do the secret water buffalo handshake with their thumbs

Contorting

In all those impossible directions.

This was long before the good words of

Hare Krishna entered

Your mind.

I hum under my breath, "Flintstones, meet the Flintstones,"

As if Hanna-Barbera is somehow stronger than Krishna,

But the traffic stops and you move on

Tapping your

Bongo

And chanting in a low, incomprehensible mumble

A piece that must surely be devotionary

But sounds so much – maybe a little too much –

Like the theme from "Gilligan's Island."

Lucy's Lucky Lighter

Lucy was down on her luck and sat in the bar that night with a pack

Of Marboros and a beer wishing her life would just end.

She pulled out a cigarette but realized she had no way to light it.

"Of course," she thought, "nothing in my life is the way I want it."

At that moment, a genie appeared on the bar stool next to her

And lit her cigarette with a beautiful, jewel-encased lighter.

"Here Lucy," he said. "Keep this lighter – it will bring great luck."

He disappeared with a poof and Lucy looked around the bar to

See if anyone had noticed the apparition that had just lit her smoke.

She looked again at the lighter and thought, "Maybe this is my lucky break."

At that moment, her friend Otto walked into the bar,

And asked for a light which she provided with the new lighter.

He then bought a lottery ticket from the machine by the pool table,

Sat down next to her and scratched off an instant win of $200,000.

The bar was celebrating when Lucy's sister Maggie strolled up with an

Unlit Virginia Slim which Lucy fired with her new lighter.

Maggie then sat down next to a stranger who turned out to be the man of

Her dreams, her soul mate, and in a month they would be married.

Ted the bartender leaned over and said, "I think you have a lucky lighter."

He pushed his unlit cigarette towards her and as soon as Lucy fired it,

The telephone rang from a New York publishing house offering a contract to

Publish a manuscript Ted had been working on his entire life.

So there was much happiness and celebration in the bar that night,

Except for Lucy, who smoked countless cigarettes but never received

Even the slightest twinge of good tidings.

She went home and smoked three packs waiting for the magic,

And continued to do so every night for six months.

In that time, Otto the lottery winner fell asleep in bed while smoking

And burned down the house he bought with his winnings,

Her sister Maggie learned she had an advanced tumor on her lung

And died three days before her three-month wedding anniversary,

And Ted the bartender developed emphysema and fell into a coma before

His novel was edited and the entire project was dropped.

And so it was that Lucy was alone with her lighter one August night

Not a bit luckier than she had been before she received the gift.

"I'm giving you one last chance, lighter," she said. "I've smoked

Ten thousand cigarettes in the last six months and no luck from you!"

She put a smoke between her lips, lit the tip and smoked it,

Waiting for a miracle.

But she had now smoked so much over the previous months that the taste

Of the nicotine made her ill and the smell of the smoke made her choke.

She finished half of the cigarette and walked over to the window

Of her sixth-floor apartment and looked once more at the lighter.

She threw it out to the street below, followed by her last pack of cigarettes.

She would never smoke again.

Lucy's lighter was indeed

Lucky.

So You Want More Eggplant?

Now that you have finished "Eggplant Rufus" – you are no doubt faced with the dilemma: "Should I throw it away?" or "Should I give it away?" Let me tell you, the best thing you can possibly do is the latter – and help spread the message of Eggplant Rufus throughout the world.

Sure, you are privileged – you have your own eggplant, but what about those friends and family who have never experienced the journey you have just accomplished? Is it fair for you to hold out on them – should they not also endure the same punishment?

The answer is a resounding "yes" – and you know it. So here are two very simple ways to acquire additional Eggplants for your friends, your family – even your enemies!

<u>On the Worldwide Web</u>: Just find your way to the internet, and check out our website: www.eggplantrufus.com At this website, you can purchase additional copies of "Eggplant Rufus" using your credit card. Each copy of Eggplant Rufus is fifteen bucks. I don't charge you for shipping, I'm just so happy to get rid of them, I will actually pay the postage to have it sent to you. There are other tidbits of information on the site you might find engaging, so spend some time – bookmark it, make it a part of your life.

<u>Through the U.S. Mail</u>: Well, if you want to do it the hard way, we can accommodate you. Simply take a piece of paper, and write your address on it. Then, after your write your address, tell us how many copies of "Eggplant Rufus" you would like. You might write something like this: "Send me ten copies of 'Eggplant Rufus.'" You might want more, you might want less. Then, take a calculator and take the number of copies you want to purchase and multiple that by fifteen dollars. Then write a check for that amount and make it payable to: EAM, Inc. Put the check and the paper with your address in an envelope and send it to:

> EAM, Inc.   54 Westerly Road   Camp Hill, PA 17011

Don't forget to put a stamp on that envelope either – the Post Office laughs when they see mail without postage, and they quite possibly do unsavory things to your envelope before they return it to you.